828.99171241009 041

Breaking Circles

CRPYK

Breaking Circles

Edited by
Britta Olinder

Gothenburg University

Dangaroo Press

First published in 1991 by Dangaroo Press for Commonwealth Studies, Gothenburg University.

Dangaroo Press

Australia: G.P.O Box 1209, Sydney, New South Wales, 2001
Denmark: Geding Søvej 21, 8381 Mundelstrup
UK: P.O. Box 186, Coventry CV4 7HG

ISBN 1-87-1049-35-0

Contents

Introduction

BRITTA OLINDER

Breaking – or broken – circles, in colourful variations, were depicted in Prafulla Mohanti's paintings exhibited on the walls of the main lecture room during the second Gothenburg conference of Commonwealth writing. The conference had no fixed theme but was open to the interests and preoccupations of its contributors. Gradually – and not surprisingly – what emerged as a common denominator was the breaking away from rules, patterns, and attitudes derived from western culture and imposed by colonial power; the breaking of pre-established circles to make it possible to confirm and celebrate the otherness, the difference of post-colonial writing.

Breaking up of the 'normal' structures of short story writing was something that was apparent in Rudy Wiebe's reading of his own work on the first afternoon; his stories set the pattern of emphasizing the diversity of life and art. The difficulty of breaking away from dominating patriarchal models was demonstrated in talks on women writers like Miles Franklin, Henry Handel Richardson and Adelaide Casely Hayford. The connection was made between the colonization of countries and the colonization of women, both of whom experience a sense of marginality as a result. In the writing of Christina Stead this issue was acted out, as John Colmer explained, in the opposing linear and circular structures of her text.

Kacke Götrick reminded us of the impossibility of judging, or even understanding, modern African plays without a thorough knowledge of the tradition they are built on and an insight into the culture out of which they have grown. On the same theme, Stephan Larsen gave us examples of a different world view as expressed in the Yoruba myths. Western categories have to be burst open to accommodate this otherness.

David Dabydeen contributed, in criticism as well as in his own poems, to the de-colonization of English through his use of Creole and his discussion of the difference achieved in the two dictions, i.e. in metropolitan and in post-colonial English. Eurocentric expectations also have to be discarded by looking at western customs and attitudes through the Indian eyes of Prafulla Mohanti or by realizing to what extent the Indian form of the novel is related to folk tales and to the puranas.

Peter Porter showed how Australian poets not only break away from the British tradition but also from American domination. Even when absorbing new avant-garde trends from anywhere in the world their poems now have a distinctive Australian tone. This is demonstrated in Peter Porter's own poems as well as in those of Vicki Raymond. Patrick White invites comments that emphasize clashes on different levels. Karin Hansson unravelled the tensions which exist between the vertical and the horizontal dimensions of the text while at the same time these divergent structures and conflicting viewpoints are what link the novels together into a unified whole; in contrast, John Colmer revealed unresolved contradictions in White's writing as well as his ambiguous relations to his own social environment, his readers and his critics.

The last article, by Britta Olinder, is an attempt at a comparative treatment, within the field of post-colonial literature, of a central issue of human experience and the variety in perceiving and expressing that universal experience.

Apart from creative writing and critical papers such as those presented here, the conference offered contributions from Lindiwe Mabuza – a passionate plea for freedom and equality in South Africa – and Grace Nichols on the near-hopeless task for a black person and a woman to get published. There were also sessions on language, on Anglophone and Francophone literatures in Africa, on Swedish criticism of African literature, and on the state of Canadian studies in Sweden. Thanks to Anna Rutherford and Prafulla Mohanti we could also see films from Australia and India.

It remains for me to express my thanks to people who assisted in various ways during the conference, particularly Eva Wallgren, Christine Räisänen and a group of helpful students; I also wish to thank Lennart Brune, Johan Hellberg and Björn Olinder for helping with the proofreading.

Generous economic help and other assistance from the University of Gothenburg, the British Council, and the Embassies of Canada and Australia is gratefully acknowledged. Magnus Bergwalls Stiftelse, the Kungl. och Hvitfeldtska Stipendieinrättningen and the Wilhelm och Martina Lundgrens Vetenskapsfond gave substantial economic support towards the printing of this book.

Seeing is Believing

RUDY WIEBE

/a/

'Why don't you just do it,' he said, 'and be done with it. Beginning, middle, end – the way stories have always been made. Go ahead, write.'

'It's so boring,' she muttered.

'It certainly isn't as boring as writing about writing.'

'I never said I wanted to write about writing.'

'Look,' he said, trying to be helpful, 'it's the way people live, in sequence, they meet and something doesn't happen and then they look at each other again or meet again and something does happen – somewhere in time, though maybe not connected, and that's a beginning and out of that happens a middle and maybe even an –'

'Dear god,' she groaned, 'it's so dull!'

'Damn it, why write at all then?'

'What else is there that's better?' she said.

/b/

Once upon a time in a land not too far away there lived a young maiden. She was intelligent and beautiful as maidens invariably are, and of course she was very unhappy. You see, her father who adored her had died while she was but a child and her stunningly beautiful though not particularly bright mother, not able to cope with the large estate her husband left her, quickly re-married. Her new husband, so considerate and courteous in courtship, turned out to be a clever brute on the make who blatantly favoured his twin sons from a previous marriage. Very soon the mother, worn out by cares in the usual patient suffering fashion, and with only slightly worse timing than intelligence, died.

It seems hardly necessary to elaborate on the fate of our heroine. Her twin step-brothers noticed her only to tease and, as they grew older, to chase her screaming around the great house. Her step-father was too occupied enlarging his enormous estate to notice anything; he simply kicked her aside when she got in his way. By the time she turned ten she was strong enough to be useful, and so she was sent to work in the barns. She carried hay and oats and water all day long to the one hundred horses stabled there, and after feeding she had to clean the aisles and gutters because of course the more those strong, beautiful animals ate, the more manure there was to shovel. Often she was so exhausted that she fell asleep on the straw in an empty stall, and one day her step-father noticed and said she might as well live there; it would save her time and probably be better for the horses. So she took her blanket and the picture of her father, which was all she owned, and cleared a small space for herself in the loft behind the hay bales. Soon she smelled so much like the stables that her step-brothers called her Barney.

As she grew older, she learned how to groom the horses as well, but of course she was never allowed to ride one. That was reserved for her stepfather and step-brothers only. Every day at ten fifteen the brothers would walk into the stables in their beautiful riding costumes, smelling like Brut or Igor, and parade down the aisle poor Barney had laboured to clean, deciding which horses they would ride. Every day.

Until one spring morning. As Barney led out their mounts, the soft sunlight flickered a particular aura about her there between the shining horses against the dark opening of the barn. The twins broke off their usual banter, and stared. Silently Barney held out the reins to them, but they did not move. It seemed they were both seeing her for the very first time.

/c/

'De-constructionists are not smart-ass, you ninny,' she said. 'They are parodic, they are trying to break down our conventional understanding of language and rebuil–'

'All language is convention, what the hell else can it be? Look, it's the one, greatest cooperative venture known to humanity, without it –'

'Aren't there a few other "cooperative ventures"!'

'Silly, I mean on such a massive scale, see, we both agree this thing is called "bed", everybody who speaks English, maybe a billion people or so agree, this is "bed", otherwise –'

'They won't ever call it "bad", not "bed", "bad"?'

'Oh, some of them will have a poor accent, sure, a small handicap but we all know what they really mean, they're just not quite able to –'

'What if I know better, I can hear exactly what I'm saying and I say it that way because I mean it, this is not "bed", it's "bad".'

'That's de-constructionist all right,' he said, 'it probably started because they're all foreigners and can't talk properly anyway and that gave them the idea, probably Frenchmen or Marxists.'

In the high glass and concrete departure area of an airport echoing with arrivals and leavings, with persons repeatedly paged but apparently never appearing to lift receivers and to be heard by an ear waiting for a voice, somewhere, there was a small circle of people. If they had faced outward they would have resembled muskoxen of the Arctic islands backed around young to confront enemies, but these faced in upon themselves: they were bending gradually closer and closer together, intent only upon the slowly tightening sphere they made. It could have been a family, a mother, a son, several daughters, a father. Between the slabs of echoing glass a film of quiet gathered about them, it might have been that the father or a daughter was leaving. Certainly none of them had the worn, devastated skin of someone recently hurled for hours near the edges of space. Perhaps the son was leaving, or a daughter and they were vainly trying one last time to look into each other's eyes, to see as they never had all of themselves at the same instant while their hands and arms groped around and beyond the person pressed against them for the next, trying to feel every bone in every individual body they suddenly knew they loved with an overwhelming conviction into the very cell circle and absolute affirmation of their own fingers meeting to clutch themselves. It seemed they should really be hollow globes, inside and outside every one of each other, to be touching each other completely at every surface in the desperate singing of all the pullulating nerves they had discovered within themselves, everywhere. Perhaps the mother was leaving.

'Will you write me a letter every day?'

'Then I'd have time for nothing but to write you letters.'

'Really?'

'A good letter, yes.'

'That would be lovely. You're a superb writer, but you've never written me an all-day letter.'

'I will write you an all-day letter, the most perfect letter possible. Immediately, I will send it to you special delivery, Express as they say, and every day you'll read it all day and it will tell you everything you want to know of me and of you and about us, it will be a letter you can read forever and never grow tired of, absolutely satisfying whenever you so much as glance at it, you could wear out the paper reading it so you better put it under glass and never touch it again until your looking wears it out, wears the letters right off the paper through glass, I will type it perfectly on an electric typewriter on hard, white paper and you can read it forever and it will –'

'What will it say, tell me, this perfect letter?'

'Have you put it under glass?'

'Yes, of course, my eyes are wearing it out. What?'

'It will say, a b c d f g h i j k l m n o p q r s t u v w x y z. And I'll sign it, perfectly.'

'Every day I should read that?'

'Yes, perfectly complete, just arrange it, whatever you want it to say.'

'I guess that's all carpenters do too, arrange lumber, or potters mud or painters paint –'

'Every day I want to say exactly what you want me to say – isn't that good? The perfect letter.'

'I couldn't even make the word "love" in your letter.'

'Why couldn't you?'

'You left out the "e".'

'What?'

'You didn't say "e".'

She hesitated a moment, then she said, 'You noticed that?'

'Yes.'

'Actually,' she said, 'I did say it, I was talking fast and I said "a b c dee f", I just ran it together a little, that's all.'

'There isn't much of a letter you can make out of the lumber of the English alphabet if you don't have an "e".'

'You're not listening to me.'

'I am, and you didn't say it; if you had written out what you said, you'd have no argument. No "please", no "remember", or "beauty", "sweetheart" ... "we" ... "love" ...'

'There's a lot of useable four letter words,' she said, 'without "e"s.'

'There is only *one* four letter word.'

'Yes,' she said, '"mama".'

'No. There is only *one* four letter word and I've never liked the smell of it. It stinks.'

'"Gold"?' she asked.

He would not answer. After a moment she spoke again, 'Could you write me a love letter without an "e"?'

He spoke then, very carefully, 'I-would-not-want-to-try.'

/f/

It was so dark they could not see each other's faces when the hunters finally heard the beaver coming. The sound of the creek running over stones played back to them from the cliffs in an endless lullaby and they stood still as trees against the willows, their shapes gone now from dark into darkness. They had been waiting so long for that quiet splash, that imperceptible breaking of surface in the pond before them that at first they could not recognize the sound for anything it might be: it seemed merely ... noise ... coming over the narrow water before them from the sand bar overgrown with willows, a small racket as if something was being dragged through willows and alder brush, an ever louder bumping between bushes. And nattering, like old workers trudging to the job and already anticipating a weekend. And then there fell into the indecipherable black sheet of water before them such a clumsy ... plop! ... one seeming bellyflop and then another, that the hunters nudged each other in astonishment, the very turns of their heads in the darkness betraying their utter incomprehension: these were the secret beaver they had never seen, whose dams measured and tiered the creek in steps between every bend and rapid where each fall weekend revealed more poplars devastated like wheatstraw, mown down and hurled against those still, temporarily standing? The hunters strained to see, still touching each other for fear one or the other would make a sound, they tilted forward into the darkness, and then they saw upon the invisible, suddenly silent water a string of starlight slowly being drawn.

'Okay, there,' one of them breathed.

A click, the black-green water surfaced in one spot of brilliant light. A beaver head there, a small blotch quickly turning and gone, the larger hump of back and tail flipping, Smack!, into a roil of water and gone, the hunters cursing each other almost aloud but unable to finish an oath before the head again surfaced, the light centred on it, and there was a tremendous CRASH. The cliffs hammered it back against their heads like clubs and the water exploded, seemed to smash in pieces out of the yellow light. And then again, an instant too late, another crash, smashing the pieces further into pieces.

'Shit!'

'Did you get the bugger?'

'Sure as hell you didn't!'

' Well I –'

'Sh-h-h...' the boy with the light hissed.

A head again; nose circling high out of the broken water. Was it the other one stupidly searching in the relentless light to smell its way into discovery, breath invisibility there?

The tremendous crashes this time were simultaneous and so overwhelming that only a clanging hammered in the hunters' heads, on and on, while the light wavered, searching over the pond. Gradually the sound of the rapids returned through iron to its gentle insistence. But there was nothing on the surface of the water. Only a dark green glister, and then white bits moving, it could have been autumn leaves; or bone.

/g/

'What were you doing the day I turned sixteen?'

'I wasn't born yet.'

'So what were you doing, November sixteen?'

'I was with my mother. Looking at a van Gogh exhibition.'

'In Canada? Where – Montreal?'

'No, Esterhazy, Saskatchewan – or maybe it was Cereal, Alberta.'

'A van Gogh exhibition in Esterhazy or Cereal?'

'Why not? They'd never had one there before.'

'I suppose not.'

'It was the first and only van Gogh exhibition to ever travel to North America and the paintings were hung at three-foot intervals all around the school gym, just at eye level, all those thick blazing golden Arles vineyards and bridges and canals and purple wheeling nights and thick corn fields, they made the gymnasium stinking of basketball and wrestling mats burn with rainbows, I was swimming in rainbow fire, turning somersaults like a porpoise in the Gulf Stream.'

'Your mother really liked it.'

'Not really. It just gave her a gut ache.'

Barney, still holding the horses' bridles, looked from one brother to the other in similar amazement. Slowly she understood that, in their own peculiar way, the twins were as beautiful as any horses she had ever seen. Their very twinishness was like a mirror, doubling the seeing of them with tiny, charming particularities.

'Hey,' one of them laughed at last, it was Astor who had a small dusting of beard, 'why don't you ... come ride with us?'

'Yes,' Charles laughed also, 'please do.'

'I've never ridden,' Barney said, even more amazed. 'I wouldn't know how.'

'We'll teach you,' the twins said together, but they really did not have to. The bodies of horses were so familiar to Barney that when she at last mounted one, she felt with her legs what she had already always known with the rest of her body. So they rode all day, and if the estate had not been so enormous they certainly would have discovered every corner of it. They rode about in silent happiness: only occasionally would their glances meet and one or the other would suddenly laugh and break into a gallop or jump across a creek or a fence, and the other two would instantly follow. The sun was almost down before they noticed that their horses were exhausted and that they themselves were hungry.

'Come to the house for tea,' Charles said.

'Yes,' Astor laughed, 'please do.'

So after they had rubbed down the horses together, they went up into the house. In the rose arbour opening off the library, they were served tea. Through the glass doors Barney could see the room she remembered better than any other of the house she had once lived in: the foldy leather chairs, the globes and maps, books scattered and stacked, the dark bookshelves to the ceiling; it was almost as if she could smell her father's pipe, the faint sweetness of it. Then she realized that the twins had bent towards her; that each was holding one of her hands!

'Let's get married,' they both exclaimed together, laughing.

Barney was puzzled. 'Which one?' she said.

'It doesn't matter,' Astor said, and Charles finished his thought, 'Not even father can tell us apart – one day Astor has the beard and the next day I do.'

'We're both exactly the same,' Astor said, 'you want to see?'

And indeed, Charles and Astor were as alike as two roses. Then they all three put their arms around each other in the rose arbour and laughed and laughed.

'It would be perfect,' Charles said.

'Come, marry us,' Astor echoed.

/i/

'Would you love me even if we weren't married?'

'You believe I love you now?'

'You just said so.'

'That was at least fifteen minutes ago.'

'But your actions haven't changed in fifteen minutes, they –'

'Actions are reflex, habitual, one's body is too lazy to discover new ones.'

'I believe you love me.'

'Good.'

'Would you love me still even if –'

'I don't know.'

'I know.'

'What do you know?'

'That I want to love you, married or not.'

'Good. I want to too.'

'So show me you love me. I want to see it, right now.'

'We've done everything seeable, a thousand times over, on three continents, or four.'

'Come on, lover, you're the one with the famous imagination, now come on!'

'How about ... this?'

'Nice, but no good. You did that on June 23rd, 1981.'

'I did? This too?'

'Hmm ... I don't think so ... not then, that was on October 2nd, 1976.'

'You're sure, never since then?'

'Never.'

'Aw sweetheart, there is nothing on earth so re-assuring as loving a computer.'

/j/

Under the quick knife, the body of the beaver slowly revealed itself. It was a knife-point unzippering, the gradual removal of a fur coat to expose a yellowish fat nakedness.

'You ever see a seal lying on a rock?' the skinner asked. 'Maybe in a zoo somewhere?'

The woman was looking at his knife with a certain abhorrent intensity; she said nothing, and since the man did not look up, he did not see the slight shake of her head, which might in any case have been no more than a suppressed shudder.

'They're a lot longer, but they have the same kind of bloated, boneless body,' the skinner continued. 'Maybe all water animals do, probably whales too, though I've never seen one. Skinned. Their skeletons are so deep inside layers of meat and fat, they don't seem to have any bones at all to look at. Look here, two and a half inches of fat, turning my big trees into fat, the bugger.'

The woman said nothing. His left hand was clenched in the roll of greasy fur and was tearing it back under the quick, short slashes of the knife; both his hands were thick with fat and blood, she could not imagine them touching her, anywhere.

'You cut a hole in it,' she said, pointing, 'there.'

'Shit!' his hands stopped and he looked up at her, grinning.

'You're watching me too close.'

'Don't you like me watching you?'

'You're the one doesn't like it,' and he bent to his work again.

'That's just a tiny cut, not like the bullet holes. I'll stretch it out carefully and you can sew it shut with two stitches. When it's dry, no one will ever notice.'

'What makes you think I'd touch that?'

'That's woman's work, sewing ... and when it's stretched and dry you have to chew it soft too, carefully day after day just chew it, till it's all soft and we can wrap it around our feet, keep warm at night.'

'All my six years of braces to chew a dry beaverskin?'

He laughed. 'What are beautiful teeth good for?' and did not look up to see her baring them at him. 'You'll make this softer than layered silk, you'll see, the inner fur so soft you'll ... did you ever make love on beaver fur?'

She bent her slender legs up against her breast, wrapped her arms around them. Her chin found its notch between her knees.

'I don't know,' she said slowly, 'if I could make love to a beaver.'

'That's not what I meant,' he said. 'That is not what I meant, at all.'

What was left of the beaver lay on its back; when she looked at it with half-shut eyes it seemed to be a pale, bloated torpedo tipped with two enormous yellow teeth and black flares of nostrils. Its tiny front legs, its powerful hind legs with their webbed claws dangled down like helpless afterthoughts. When she opened her eyes wide, it looked like nothing but a plastic bag of bruised fat.

'No language is translatable.'

'You're exactly wrong, the genius of language is that it is eminently translatable.'

'No, it isn't. Every language has its own systems of meaning, of reflecting what you see. If you have no past tense in a language, you cannot think about pasts.'

'That's exactly where de-constructionists so-called become so ridiculous. They take words with fine, perfectly ordinary meanings and break them up so you can't recognize the most usual – "desiring" becomes "de-siring", a beautiful word like "ineffable" becomes an obscenity contorted into a title like "Effing the Ineffable". It's dreadful.'

'That has nothing to do with what I was saying; and aren't your examples rather tendentious?'

'So what's tendentious? These so-called writers use the accidents of phonemology to get their tendentious meanings, usually obscene, into –'

'All words are play.'

'Don't jack around too. I'm talking about phonemes, sounds, not phenomes, facts.'

'I know,' she said. 'All words are play.'

'You're being ridiculous too! Words are the way human beings handle reality. You can make a game out of eating, but if you don't eat at all, you're dead.'

'I agree. Words are the deadliest game of all.'

'See, you're at it again, jacking around with words, once you start there's no stopping. It's like when you start to look for risque shapes, soon everything longer than it is wide is phallic, everything rounded is a breast –'

'Everything with a round opening, vaginal.'

'Exactly, so take it one step further, to translations.'

'I thought we agreed, languages are not translatable.'

'We didn't agree! If that thing can be "the slipper", it can certainly be "die Pantoffel" as well.'

'It's "der".'

'What?'

'It's "der Pantoffel".'

'Okay okay, German expert, now, you're taking a boat cruise down the Rhine and you buy a card showing the Lorelei and you write me in Canada, "Hey lover, here I am sailing down the River Clean and we've just passed the Laurel's Egg" ... isn't that ridiculous?'

'Hey, that's pretty good.'

'It's a joke, a silly meaningless joke based on phoneme accidents!'

'Actually, I find it ironically meaningful, really, the River Clean, I'll never –'

'Oh for pete's sake!'

'I'll never see that abused river the same way again, my sweet, and who is pete, eh?'

'The old pete, I'm sure, black with a glowing red pitchfork.'

'Oh ... I thought you had a pete – r.'

'Probably, and you no doubt have a hairy!'

'Isn't she nice?'

'Oh for –'

/n/

At first they could not believe it, but the fact was that the streets of the town were so narrow between overwhelming walls of whitewashed stone that they could not walk two abreast. Then they simply laughed; if anyone met them they would have to turn past each other sideways.

But fortunately they met no one as the cobblestones, rough as if gathered from a field, led them downwards towards the centre in the gradual evening and they were so excited by this ancientness, this definite Before Christ antiquity still being lived in in a clustered town they had glimpsed like a white-tiled splotch against a cove of the blue Mediterranean; so ecstatic at their own nerve of turn-

14

ing away from their planned route and leaving their car locked in the shadow of a wall and just walking (they had seen immediately there was no question of driving down this topless tunnel), leaving the technological safety of their car and just walking with nothing but their handbags (*Never* leave your money or passport anywhere) firmly tucked under their arms; neither was even wearing stockings, just a loose cotton dress for the heat, and sandals.

They met no one. Perhaps it was time for the evening meal; they could hear voices and kettles, pots through open windows too high to look into but letting in, at last, the evening coolness though they were still perspiring from the tremendous sun all day, and then turning a corner they saw people passing far below them where it seemed another street perhaps as narrow as their own crossed; but when they got there, laughing to themselves a little in anticipation, they were still alone.

'Make your photos?'

It was a moment before either realized they had been spoken to; in English. In any case, the intersection would have forced them to decide in which of five directions to face here where the cobblestones emerged out of their straight narrowness and circled about themselves. Even the untrained soles of their feet could feel that; if they had been blind, if the whole town were blind, the circled stones would tell them exactly where they were; and then the tops of their feet felt suddenly cold as if along one of the streets a breath had come up from the sea. A man was standing in the fold of one wall. And then they realized that it was he who had spoken to them. A square camera, was it actually of wood?, stared at them, its black cloth draped over his arm.

'Oh!' the shorter woman said, frightened. 'Oh ... I ...'

'It's much too dark,' the other woman said with complete technological assurance.

'No,' the man said without moving and without inflection. And indeed the lens at the centre of the wooden face seemed to flicker, it clicked precisely even as they stood turned slightly away from it, their lower bodies poised as it seemed for flight and their faces caught exposed, perhaps quite open. His left hand moved, presenting a piece of paper.

'Oh no you don't,' the other woman said. 'We're driving on immediately, we're not staying anywhere to pick up a picture tomorrow, we're not going to be pressured by some unscrupulous –'

But the paper already in her hand was the picture. She recognized herself in bright sunlight: her back, she was getting out of a taxi in front of her own suburban house and there were her three tall children running, it seemed they were running down the curved walk to greet her!

She could not believe what she saw in her hand, her three children, their faces...

'Where's mine?' the shorter woman demanded beside her.

The man had glanced once at the picture he had taken and now he quickly shook his head. 'No,' he said, crouching back as if he would have been happy to disappear into the wall, 'it is not good, no.'

'Where's John?' the other woman said, still staring at the picture.

'You're a fake!' the shorter woman spit out, 'You're all alike, fakes trying to get money out of us, well, what do I look like in front of my house, eh, show me! Come on!'

But the picture she received did not show her. There was no person on it at all. Only the straight walk between the two birches leading to the front door of her house. There was no one there at all.

'There's just the three kids,' the other woman said, still staring.

'I did not want to take it,' the man said to the shorter woman, his face hunched painfully together; his voice so deeply gentle, almost as if he were praying the miserere.

'Where's my John!' the other woman screamed.

They stood side by side feeling the circular stones under their unwilling feet. They had not even planned to visit this town, their car was waiting for them, with one slight twist of a key it would carry them instantly, permanently away. But here they felt the stones, revelations laid before their defenseless eyes.

/o/

'Please, don't do that.'

'Sweetheart, I want to talk to you about it.'

'Why?'

'Because I like it, I want to experience more of −'

'Then why not just read it again?'

'I will, I will.'

'Readers nowadays are such meaning hounds, sniffing, sniffing after nothing but meaning, yes, I get a whiff here, there's a spoor of meaning, sniff, sniff ... if that was all there was to meaning a writer could just make one big stink and be done with it: the husband is a son of a bitch! Period!'

'It means a lot more then − okay, I'm not looking for meanings, it just *is*, okay? But ... why did you arrange the parts in the order you did?'

'I don't know.'

'Look, I don't believe that, when you write you're so careful you −'

'That's why they're labelled "a", "b", "c" etc. − you can read them in any order you please.'

'But "b" comes after "a", and "h" always before "j", so−'

'Not when you write words they don't.'

'What? Are you trying to make a word out of −'

'Read them in any order you please, only please!'

'A story has to have a pattern!'

'Not necessarily. It could be − a necklace, with various beads in a relationship to each other, that's all.'

'Then ... I don't see the string.'

'Why do you have to see it? You sense perhaps it's there, somewhere at the centre of things, but in good necklaces you never see the string, only individual beads juxtaposed. Don't be so damned logical!'

'Okay, the true beauty of a necklace is brought out when it is hung around a neck, right? So whe–'

'Right! You're the neck.'

'Me?'

'Yes you. You've read my story, you're wearing the necklace.'

'Oh. Has it ...' he hesitated, then plunged on, 'Was it, has it made me beautiful? '

'You always are,' she said, suddenly moved by a profound love. 'I don't really know, about the necklace. Maybe you don't need it.'

'But I *want* it.'

'I know. But maybe the story isn't really a necklace. Maybe it's just a ... a random scatter of beads, as spilled on a bed.'

'Not a "bad"?'

'No, bed, b-e-d, bed.'

'Of course,' he laughed. 'If you want to, right away.'

Adelaide Casely Hayford: A Founding Mother the Cosmopolitan Way

KIRSTEN HOLST PETERSEN

Memoirs are not just stories of what happened and did not happen in the course of a particular lifetime, they also represent the writer's self image, her past life carefully arranged according to a vision or a plan, and they have a pattern forced upon them by the genre itself. For those reasons they are unreliable as guides to the life they portray. A picture of the ideas and personality of Adelaide Casely Hayford can be gained from her memoirs as well as her few short stories and articles, but one has to listen to the tone of voice of the written words in order to get to know the personality behind the memoirs, and one also has to be aware of the larger historical and ideological setting of the life in order to assess the ideas.

A convenient starting point is to find out what other people, preferably her contemporaries, thought about her. At the age of eighty-five, Adelaide Casely Hayford wrote her memoirs, for serialization in *West Africa Review*,[1] a monthly where they appeared between October 1953 and August 1954. In the caption which announces the beginning of the series, *West Africa Review* calls her 'a wonderful lady whose like has not occurred before in West Africa.

- The last of her era and the last of her kind.'[2] The first part sounds blandly pleasant and the second part sounds vaguely mystical, but the touch of sensationalism is obviously prompted by the magazine's interest in catching the readers' attention, so the opinion of *West Africa Review* can not be trusted altogether. Sir George Beresford-Stook, KCMG, Crown Agent and lately Governor of Sierra Leone (this long title is due to the constitutional changes Sierra Leone was going through in preparation for Independence in 1961) was prevailed upon to write a foreword to the memoirs and he talks about 'her personal charm, her wonderful vitality and vivacity and the aristocracy of her intellect', and he ends by calling her 'the great little lady with the large heart, who has done so much for others with so little thought for herself'.[3] That frankly sounds appalling, but again the banal language and the fulsome praise could well say more about Sir George than about Adelaide Casely Hayford. A more sober tone is struck in her obituary in the same journal in 1960, where her nephew, Dr M.C.F. Easmond, talks about her 'sunny and happy nature' and calls her 'one of Sierra Leone's most remarkable personalities'.[4] Obituaries, of course, have their own rules, the most important of which surely is to pay tribute to the deceased and thus praise her; but another law of obituaries is that they are only written about persons who by common consent are felt to be special in some way. It is that specialness which this paper attempts to grasp and assess.

Not withstanding the obituary and Crown Agent praise, many people will be unfamiliar with Adelaide Casely Hayford, so I shall start by giving an outline of the events that shaped her life. Adelaide Casely Hayford was born in 1868 in Freetown in Sierra Leone, the granddaughter on her father's side of an English Chief Justice who had married the daughter of a Fantee chief. Her mother was in Adelaide Casely Hayford's own words the daughter of an 'illiterate Mandingo trader' and a man who was a descendant of the Maroons, a group of West Indian slaves who had revolted against their masters and eventually arrived in Freetown in 1800. Adelaide was thus coloured rather than black, and she refers to herself as a 'Hamite', which she appears to resent, as she is envious of some of her sisters who were of lighter complexion and therefore got 'all the cream' whilst the others 'subsist[ed] on skimmed milk'.[5] Her father was the registrar of the Court of Mixed Commissions in Sierra Leone, a body which dealt with slave owners and tried to reunite scattered liberated slave families. They had eight children of which Adelaide was the sixth, and on her father's retirement when Adelaide was four years old the family went to live in England to give the children an English or 'good' education. When Adelaide was twelve she was enrolled in the Jersey Ladies' College from which she graduated four years later with a School Certificate. In the pursuit of further education she was sent to Germany, partly to learn German and partly to study music at a branch of the Stuttgart Conservatory. She spent a couple of years in Germany but was forced to go back to England because of lack of money. 1892-93 find her teaching in Freetown for a short spell, but she returned to England and only came to settle in Freetown in 1897 because that had been her father's dying wish. She felt alien and was met with hostility, and in 1900 she was back in England, supporting herself and her sisters by running a boarding house for bachelors.

It was during this time that she received a 'very short letter' in which the orthography was 'a bit doubtful' from a Gold Coast lawyer, Joseph Ephraim Casely Hayford, asking permission to visit her, and they were married in London in 1903. Casely Hayford rose to be the most eminent West African lawyer, nationalist and politician of his time, but Adelaide hated her various stays in small towns on the Gold Coast, where he practised. She took her baby daughter Gladys to England for medical treatment and on her return tried to settle in Cape Coast, 'which in those days was by far the best spot for an educated woman on the Gold Coast'.[6] It was obviously not good enough, because in 1914 she separated from her husband and went to live and teach in Freetown. She was consumed with a passion to open a girls' vocational school for 'the uplift of our womanhood'. With that in mind she collected and borrowed money to go to America to visit vocational schools there. Between 1920 and 1923 she and her niece travelled all over America, visiting and speaking at such famous schools as Tuskegee College (Booker T. Washington's school), Hampton University, and Atlanta University where Du Bois taught, and addressing an endless number of mainly coloured, but also white congregations up and down the country with the aim of collecting money and setting up funds both for her own return ticket and for the school, which opened in Freetown in 1923. Mrs Casely Hayford was now fifty-five years old. In 1925 she made a second visit to America which appears to have been as great a success as the first visit and brought funds to continue the school. She ran the school and taught domestic science classes until 1940 when age forced her to close the school.

During the Twenties and Thirties Mrs Casely Hayford was a well-known and controversial public figure in Freetown. She was known for wearing national costume, even when receiving distinguished guests, like the Prince of Wales, when every other woman in town was trying to 'beg, borrow or steal gloves for the grand reception'. Her main interest remained the education of girls, and she herself provided an example of an educated and independent woman who supported herself and her daughter at a time when this was most unusual. She was a frequent visitor at Government House, and in 1935 she received the Silver Jubilee Medal, and she rounded it off with an MBE in 1949, at the age of eighty-one, just four years before she wrote her memoirs in *West Africa Review*, and eleven years before she died in 1960.

These dates and names provide just the bare bones of a life, but certain aspects can already be deduced from them. She was obviously a well-travelled and cosmopolitan person; she writes in her memoirs that she has crossed the sea to England twenty-one times, so she knows what she is talking about when she discusses conditions during the passage. Her ideas centre around the two major themes of cultural nationalism and education for girls, and she must have been a person of unusual determination and energy to pack that amount of travel and personal achievement into one life, even such a long one as hers. Before getting any closer to the person and ideas behind the memoirs, however, a word of warning about the perspective and circumstances of the memoirs is in order.

West Africa Review was a monthly magazine, and Adelaide Casely Hayford's memoirs appear consecutively from October 1953 to August 1954. That makes eleven instalments, of which ten are of roughly equal length, and one is considerably shorter, leading one to suspect that ten instalments was the aim, but that one of them became too long and was shared rather unequally between two issues. The first seven instalments move consecutively forward in time, each taking in between one year and twenty years, dependent on how important the particular time appeared to the writer. They end in 1935 with a visit to England. The next three chapters are organized thematically rather than chronologically, and they consist of a profile of Adelaide Casely Hayford's daughter, Gladys Casely Hayford, a recollection of the important people Adelaide Casely Hayford had met, and a profile of the Governors of Sierra Leone whom she had met and known. The last instalment predictably discusses briefly the moment of writing, the writer's present, and then moves on to considerations for the future.

This pattern of serialization forces its own pattern onto the material. Each instalment must include a highlight, a journey to somewhere interesting or a meeting with a particularly famous person. This tends to give the impression of a hop from one high point to another when the memoirs are read at one sitting. Criticism and opposition are left behind, and the persona always emerges victorious. The distortions which lie behind this view can, of course, also be intended, as they would vindicate the persona in the eyes of readers who are assumed to be hostile, and Adelaide Casely Hayford must have been aware, as she wrote the memoirs, that the readership of *West Africa Review* included people or relatives of people she had at one time antagonized in her advocacy of cultural nationalism or in clashes over fund raising for her school. This adaptation of the literal truth, however, becomes the undeniable proof of another kind of truth, namely the spirit of the persona, who brings that fighting spirit she describes into the very structure of the memoirs. The serial form with its large and varied readership can thus be said to support Adelaide Casely Hayford's polemic purposes and, behind that, suit her combatative and assertive personality.

Another perspective which has to be taken into account is Adelaide Casely Hayford's great age at the time of writing the memoirs (she was eighty-five). One obvious aspect of this is the fact that most of the people she mentions are dead at the time of writing, and she has an obsession with pointing this out, even when it is not relevant to what she is talking about. Thus, when talking about a member of her family, Joseph Spilbury Smith, whose main problem was that he kept failing his final exam in medicine and therefore became a terrible drain on the family income, she leaves behind the time she is describing, which is her childhood, in order to tell us that he eventually 'joined the government service, being sent to Tarkwa ... where he filled the dual capacity of doctor and District Commissioner, and where he died'.[7] Looked at from the end of a long life, time evidently shrinks. There is a ten-year gap between the sixth and the seventh instalment, presumably nothing much happened, but in contrast to that the seventh instalment covers only one year, or rather one trip to England, which obviously looms larger in the writer's memory. The principle of selection is always subjective in memoirs, but to Adelaide Casely Hayford time disappears down a tunnel of almost a century, and people come and go like generations, and it is almost inevitable that she should sit above them, in judgement. In most cases, she has the final word.

This, however, does not imply that she is in some way timeless; on the contrary, she is very much set in time. Her problem is rather that she is writing out of the sensibility of a previous age. This has the obvious result of her complaining about modern times and modern girls who are 'blasé' and 'devoid of any racial altruism and patriotism, and seem to be out simply to benefit themselves'.[8] She admits frankly and rather movingly in the last instalment that writing the memoirs has helped her distinguish between then and now and, 'in all honesty, I must confess, I prefer the "then" to the "now". Everybody feels that way. It is a universal preference.'[9]

If one was to try to set the 'then' in time, I think it would be the period from 1900 to the early Twenties, which is when Adelaide Casely Hayford through her husband came into close contact with the cultural nationalism which became such an important part of her message and also the period when she took the message to America with such success and when she realized her dream of a vocational school for girls. These achievements set her apart from, and often in opposition to, the creole élite on the West Coast of Africa of which she was an integral part and whose ethos had shaped her sensibility and aspirations.

The memoirs begin and close with genealogies of relatives, and this framework of genealogies is a good indication of Adelaide Casely Hayford's social aspirations, or perhaps rather the class she wishes to be associated with. Seeing that the place is Freetown and the time somewhere in the first quarter of the nineteenth century, the first ancestor will obviously be a liberated slave, but after one or at the most two generations we meet the following people amongst her relatives:

> ... with the exception of the youngest, Francis – the first African barrister – who eventually became a Puisne Judge in the Gold Coast, they were all more or less settled in life... One of the sons – Robert – became one of the first qualified doctors in Africa, and entered the Government Service. He married the daughter of Sir Benjamin Chilley Pine, the Governor of the Gambia... Twin sisters – Phillipa and Mary – both married doctors... Mary became the wife of Surgeon Major Davies, one of the two black men who were recognised in the military service at the time. Most of their decendants are occupying good positions in Freetown today: among them the Clintons, the Wrights, [etc.][10]

Adelaide Casely Hayford's concern with titles comes across as straightforward snobbery and the apex of her social universe is the professions, lawyers and doctors. In this she is in tune with creole aspirations, particularly in the first two decades. The Creole society in Freetown consisted of waves of immigrants from England and the West Indies, the Black Poor and the Maroons, intermarried with liberated slaves after the Slave Trade Act in 1807. The special circumstances of this society attracted missionaries, both white and Afro-American, and they set about christianizing and civilizing the liberated slaves. They also tried to persuade them to start an agricultural production, along Buxton's lines of 'the bible and the plough', but memories of slave labour initially made the immigrants unwilling to take this path, and as trade quickly showed itself to be both easier and more lucrative, Freetown came to be a society of traders. The protestant ethos of the Methodists and the C.M.S. (Church Missionary Society) helped in this process, and an educational report from 1841 states that 'Multitudes of them are yearly passing from the condition of predial labourers to that of petty traders and artisans'.[11] The Victorian capitalist virtues of thrift, industry, self-reliance, initiative and religious fervour seem to have lifted the liberated slaves out of a state which they themselves came to regard as barbarous. The Freetown version of the rags-to-riches dream was slave to petty trader to rich merchant, and the cultural expressions of this were emulation of Western habits and thought patterns, leadership in church and perhaps in politics as an unofficial member of the Legislative Council. To the rich merchants in leading positions towards the end of the 19th century, there was, however, yet another rung on the ladder, the professions, the ultimate in Western education, so their sons tended to go to England to study rather than take over the family firm. They were the black Englishmen, dressed like the schoolmaster J.E. Casely Hayford describes in his autobiographical novel *Ethiopia Unbound*:

> In his elegantly cut-away black morning coat and beautifully-glazed cuffs and collar, not to speak of patent leather shoes, which he kept spotlessly bright by occasionally dusting them with his pocket handkerchief, tucked away in his shirt sleeves, he certainly looked a swell, but he also looked a veritable fool.[12]

The top layer of this society has been described as 'been-to, jaguar and frightful'.[13] They were initially praised for Christian endeavour, but, as Coleman put it, 'it is psychologically difficult for a model to regard an imitator as his equal'[14] and by 1900 there had been a definite change in the British attitude to the Creoles and they were relegated to inferior positions in the Civil Service, whilst the Chiefs of the native people in the Protectorate were looked to as future leaders. The Creoles suffered from this dilemma of acceptance and rejection, and an opposition arose and crystallized in E.W. Blyden's authorship as cultural nationalism. To him, races had distinct and different characteristics, and the black race was important in God's overall plan as compensation for the arrogance of the white race. African cultural habits in dress, speech, food, religion and institutions should therefore be respected, and if they were,

Ethiopia would 'rise from her slumber' and once more gain the height of her former splendour, as in ancient Egypt. Islam and polygamy were special African expressions of culture. J.E. Casely Hayford supported these ideas and popularized them in *Ethiopia Unbound*, and he also sought to put them into practice in both legal and political work, but despite the often violent rhetoric of the cultural nationalist movement, they were not revolutionaries. The methods chosen to further their aims were petitions, lawsuits and memberships of boards and councils.

Adelaide Casely Hayford's version of cultural nationalism fits snugly into traditional ideas of a woman's world. To a large extent she ignores the philosophical aspects of the movement and concentrates on the physical, tangible everyday expressions of it. She translates Blyden's African personality into a question of wearing national dress because 'it would be so much more picturesque ... and would show that we were proud of being Africans'. In talking about the aims of her school, she wishes to instill into the girls 'love of country, a pride of race, an enthusiasm for a black man's capabilities and a genuine admiration for Africa's wonderful art at work'. She sees the girls 'sitting in homes which combined European order, method and cleanliness with the beauty of native basket furniture, art work and draperies', and when this mixture of 'what is good in European education and the natural heritage of African individuality' has been achieved, she can picture the sons and daughters of Africa's race 'looking the whole world in the face ... with such self-respect as to command the respect of all other nations'.[15] It is difficult to consider these statements controversial, but in fact they are hedged in with controversy at either end of the scale of conservative-radical thinking. Polite Creole society was offended by the outward signs, particularly the native dress. One of the phrases which are repeated in the memoirs is 'truly a prophet is without honour in his own country',[16] and she states dryly about the reception of her school: 'Had I been starting a brothel, the antagonism could not have been worse.'[17] She was forced to drop the idea of wearing national dress at school and also to change the syllabus to include more academic subjects, which downgraded the vocational aspect which was the essence of her educational ideas.

At the radical end of the scale she was not willing to take the full consequences of her ideas, and this involved her in some contradictions. She wanted to teach native basketry at her school, but as the native women who could do this 'cannot be relied upon for systematic labour', she sent someone reliable, i.e. 'civilized', into the bush to learn it. She shared Creole society's contempt for the natives and she had no problem in separating symbolic recognition (her admiration for native basketry and dress) from its object (native, tribal society). To put this into perspective, however, one could look at the play which won the drama competition for the celebration of Independence in 1961, R. Sarif Easmon's play *Dear Parent and Ogre*.[18] Set in very upper-class Creole society in Freetown, it swims in champagne and deals in trips to Paris, Cadillacs and picnics of French splendour, and ideologically it advocates a very cautious anti-tribalism. Seen in this context Adelaide Casely Hayford's contradictory views thirty-five years earlier appear understandable, even laudable, as they show that she had left the safe shore of approved opinion (a firm contempt for everything 'tribal') and therefore faced difficulties which were evidently not easily solved.

But cultural nationalism was only one aspect of the ideas surrounding the vocational school for girls. Another aspect which tended to clash with the cultural nationalism was her view of the role of women and hence the education of girls.

Education as such is one of the main features of the growth of Freetown. Initially seen as the most effective instrument of 'civilization' it quickly became the crowning ambition of the freed slaves, and already in 1840 there were forty-two schools in Freetown. Education was for a long time in the hands of missionaries. In 1845 the C.M.S. opened a Grammar school for boys and in 1849 a secondary school for girls. One of the main aims of the cultural nationalists was to create an African university which would teach courses relevant to African students. In 1876 Fourah Bay College, which had been refounded in 1827 by the C.M.S. to train teachers and missionaries, was affiliated to Durham University and changed its curriculum accordingly.

True to the dichotomy between the world of men and women, J.E. Casely Hayford spent his energy advocating an African university whilst Adelaide Casely Hayford worried about the education of children; or rather girls. Her use of the word 'vocational' is somewhat ambiguous. Her main aim was to teach the girls 'the responsibilities of motherhood; the care of children; the comfort of the husband and the duties of the home'.[19] For this purpose she visited the 'school for brides' which Booker T. Washington's wife had added to Tuskagee. If one looks at her ideas in the light of the educational development of Freetown, she is very much in line with the reports of various commissions, set up to investigate the situation, and with their recommendations which were in the main for a more vocational direction and a movement away from the heavy insistence on religion.

In terms of the values of Creole society, the role she visualized for women was very acceptable in that it was a direct imitation of Victorian values; but to the Creole mind she devalued this aim by wanting the girls to take an interest in native arts and crafts. Society did not share her interest in cultural nationalism. In terms of feminism, one has to conclude, her ideal woman is 'The Angel in the House'. This ideal was for her embodied in Sarah Halloway, a white American millionairess and philanthropist, whom she found 'an absolute saint; impregnating the very walls of her beautiful home with an atmosphere of love;

goodwill and unforgettable selfishness. She simply radiated kindness.'[20] This is the very image which the English suffragettes had battled against several decades before Adelaide Casely Hayford embraced it. To add a further complexity to this picture, Adelaide Casely Hayford's own life was very far from this perceived ideal. She obviously lacked the submissiveness necessary for the role; she was in fact an independent professional woman supporting herself and her daughter. But her ideas, conservative and mild as they appear, were radical compared to those of her husband who, in *Ethiopia Unbound*, describes his proposal of marriage to his first wife who died, but who was obviously the love of his life. She tells him that she has been offered the post of headmistress of the junior classes of the home university, and he replies: 'How can you think of such a thing?' However, when soothed by her feminine charm, he takes hold of her hands and exclaims: 'It has often occurred to me that the child-like hand that shall guide me through life's labyrinthine ways is the self same one that I now hold tenderly in my own.'[21]

This may be a moving scene, but it is very far from Adelaide Casely Hayford's reality, as is his advocacy of polygamy and his comment after the marriage of one of his characters, 'and none of his wives sought to be leaders of their society',[22] which of course is exactly what Adelaide Casely Hayford strove to become. My point in setting her opinion between these various points of view is to show that she found herself in an ideological no-woman's land where she had different ideas from her contemporaries, but on the other hand cannot be said to be the forerunner of later women's movements.

She combined her idea of cultural nationalism with the Victorian image of women, but she clearly preferred the Victorian Christian aspect of the combination. In her short story 'Mr Courifer', the hero, Mr Courifer, is a cultural nationalist. He lives in a mud hut and wears national costume, but he expresses a clear preferance for English family life. 'I like to see mother and father and the little family sitting down eating their meal together.'[23] This obviously clashes with Blyden's and Casely Hayford's image of the polygamous family which they saw as essential to an authentic African way of life, but it is also unaffected by the suffragette movement in England where she grew up, and also by the American movement to gain the vote. She was present at the yearly national convention of Coloured Women in Indianapolis in 1920 where, according to herself, she 'arrived, saw and conquered' in her picturesque native costume. She had postcards made of herself and her niece, and they 'sold like hot loaves',[24] but she has nothing to say about the ideas which were discussed on that important occasion. She thus seems to end up in the unenviable position of being an extremely embattled woman in her lifetime, but at the same time she failed to emerge as the forerunner of the main development of African nationalism or of the women's movement.

Despite her vast travel experiences she seems curiously unaware of the important events of history which directly shaped her destiny and which were much debated issues in nationalist circles. She mentions World War I because her sister travelled on a ship which was torpedoed, and she mentions the Bai Bureh uprising, an insurrection against the imposition of hut taxes in the Protectorate, and here she takes the view of the missionaries that it was a revolt against civilization! Again she is not so much concerned with the issues – she does not even mention the hut tax – but with relatives who might get killed. She can perhaps be excused for being in Germany in 1885 without mentioning the Berlin conference, but when she selects for recounting an incident where the Kaiser visits a finishing school and his wife chooses to address a few words to her cousins, probably because they were dark, it becomes emblematic of the way she perceives life around her. She is in America, staying in Harlem in 1920-21; and yet she manages to not notice the rallies in which Marcus Garvey brought more black people together in a show of race solidarity than had ever been done before. They were not her kind of people. Instead she gets into personal contact with some of New York's 'exclusive 400' and one of them tells her – according to herself – that she has 'made an exceedingly good impression on the very best people in America'.[25] Alice Walker's black America is completely invisible on these triumphant tours through America.

One thing there can be no doubt about is her tremendous strength of character, and this any group or period must grant her. For a start she had a mean line in backhanded compliments. Her childhood, she tells us, was characterized by spontaneous happiness and joy 'in spite of rigid discipline and somewhat spartan methods'.[26] About her mother she 'can never remember her playing with us ... she spent her days more or less on a luxurious sofa'.[27] Sharing was a great feature of her home, 'even eggs were shared, spread upon thick pieces of breadscrape'.[28] The first time she taught in Freetown, she taught under a Mr James Taylor, 'a prominent trader, whose capacity for business entirely eclipsed his capacity for training girls'.[29]

Her most devastating remarks, however, are reserved for the instalment called 'Profile of Gladys', a tribute to her (deceased) daughter. According to that, Gladys was 'in a chronic state of financial embarrassment; largely brought about by her marriage (without my knowledge) to a man I had never seen; and who was never able to support her and their little boy'. In addition to that little slip, Gladys apparently had no sense of values, neither of human beings nor of commodities, and when she goes to Europe this has the effect which probably most mothers, along with Adelaide Casely Hayford, fear, 'her lack of discrimination prompted her to choose to join a coloured jazz troupe with headquarters in Berlin. She bitterly regretted her decision in after years.'[30] As usual, Adelaide Casely Hayford has the last word. I for one would not choose her for a mother.

With those remarks about her daughter she has also absolved us from the duty to not speak ill of the dead. In the last installment of her memoirs she sums herself up, saying that 'she had tremendous conceit; had been a bit of a snob; a very poor loser, a procastinator and most of all, her main failing was her "Napoleonic spirit of domination"',[31] and to this she adds rather disarmingly that this is 'generally true of very short people; who want to make up in importance for the inches they lack in stature'. Although modesty and the genre demand these confessions, they seem to be true; with the ironic addition that she was tremendously immodest, not to say boastful.

On a less personal level, although she does not seem a complex person in herself, an assessment of her is difficult. The reason for this is to be found in the way in which her ideas fall in between accepted codes and new developments. She must be given credit for the courage to be out of phase with her society and for adhering to her opinions in adversity, but she falls short of being given the honour of a founding mother because some of her ideas, particularly those concerned with education and the role of women, had been overtaken, even in her own lifetime. This position which I have referred to as an ideological no-woman's-land also adds to the difficulty of assessing her. One could choose to condemn one aspect of her or extoll another, and the fact that she comes across as an immensely snobby and a not particularly likeable person is a further restriction on objectivity. Perhaps one can conclude that a 'difficult personality' or a 'Napoleonic spirit of domination' are inevitable characteristics of a person who shakes her society out of indolence by shocking it, but that ironically – because this was part of what she fought against – Creole snobbery and her own excessive admiration for not just English, but Victorian values clouded her vision so that the scope of that vision fell short of the admirable energy with which she pursued it.

NOTES

1. *West Africa Review* (West African Graphic Co. Ltd., London). Referred to in Notes as *WAR*.
2. *WAR*, October 1953, p. 1058.
3. Ibid., p. 1058.
4. *WAR*, 1960, p. 52.
5. *WAR*, October 1953, p. 1059.
6. *WAR*, December 1953, p. 1311.
7. *WAR*, October 1953, p. 1059.
8. *WAR*, March 1954, p. 241.
9. *WAR*, August 1954, p. 789.
10. *WAR*, October 1953, p. 1059.
11. Christopher Fyfe, *Sierra Leone Inheritance* (London, 1964).
12. J.E. Casely Hayford, *Ethiopia Unbound* (London, 1969), p. xxviii.
13. A.T. Porter, *Creoldom: A Study of the Development of Freetown Society* (OUP, London, 1963), p. 69.
14. James S. Coleman, *Background to Nationalism* (University of California Press, Berkeley, 1958), p. 147.
15. Adelaide Casely Hayford, 'A Girls' School in West Africa' in *Southern Workman*, Vol. 55, October 1926, p. 450.
16. Ibid., p. 451.
17. *WAR*, March 1954, p. 241.
18. R. Sarif Easmon, *Dear Parent and Ogre* (Oxford University Press, London, 1964).
19. Adelaide Casely Hayford, 'A Girls' School in West Africa', p. 449.
20. *WAR*, March 1954, p. 243.
21. *Ethiopia Unbound*, p. 34.
22. Ibid., p. 210.
23. Adelaide Casely Hayford, 'Mista Courifer', in *Unwinding Threads. Writing by Women in Africa*, edited by Charlotte H. Brunner (Heinemann, London, 1983), p. 15.
24. *WAR*, January 1954, p. 57.
25. *WAR*, March 1954, p. 243.
26. *WAR*, October 1953, p. 1059.
27. *WAR*, October 1953, p. 1059.
28. *WAR*, October 1953, p. 1060.
29. *WAR*, December 1953, p. 1305.
30. *WAR*, May 1954, p. 415.
31. *WAR*, August 1954, p. 735.

Yoruba Mythology in the Works of Wole Soyinka

STEPHAN LARSEN

Wole Soyinka, the famous Nigerian author, is a Yoruba. The importance of Yoruba traditions to his writing has been pointed out by several of those who have analyzed his works, e.g. Eldred Jones in *The Writing of Wole Soyinka* (London, 1973), Gerald Moore in *Wole Soyinka* (London and Ibadan, 1978), and Oyin Ogunba in *The Movement of Transition: A Study of the Plays of Wole Soyinka* (Ibadan, 1975). My object in this essay is to give a few examples of how, and to what purpose, Soyinka uses Yoruba myths in his literary texts.

The Yoruba gods are numerous; about 400, according to some sources.[1] To Soyinka, the most important of them all appears to be Ogun, the god of metals, creativity and war. Ogun aids and protects anyone who uses metal tools or handles metals in his daily work. He is the god of soldiers, hunters, blacksmiths, engineers, lorry-drivers, barbers, butchers, wood-carvers and surgeons, among others. Being a lover of truth, he supervises all sorts of oaths and pacts. It is very usual for followers of Ogun to cement pacts of friendship at a smithy and to demonstrate their intention of speaking the truth, e.g. in a court of law, by kissing a piece of iron.

According to one of the best known myths of Ogun, he was the one who made way for the other gods when, in the beginning of time, they wanted to go down to the newly-created earth in order to take possession of it. Having completed this difficult and dangerous task of his, Ogun retired to Mount Idanre, where he lived in isolation for a long period of time. However, he eventually let himself be persuaded by a delegation from the town of Ire to lead the soldiers of Ire in battle against the army of a neighbouring town. This resulted in a terrible massacre, for in the heat of battle, Ogun was so blinded by rage and blood lust, that he could not tell his allies from his enemies, but completely wiped out his own army. This myth clearly demonstrates the duality of Ogun's character - he is at the same time a self-sacrificing pioneer and a brutal warrior, his power is both life-giving and lethal.

Ogun affects the chain of events, directly or through human agents, in nine of Soyinka's fourteen published plays and in both his novels. In Soyinka's poetry, too, the presence of this dynamic god can be felt.

Ogun himself appears in three works: the drama *A Dance of the Forests* (London and Ibadan, 1963), and the long poems 'Idanre' (in *Idanre and Other Poems*, London, 1967) and *Ogun Abibimañ* (London and Ibadan, 1976). In the drama *The Road* (London and Ibadan, 1965), there is a character, Murano, who is completely controlled by Ogun, unable to act of his own accord. This Murano, about whom more will be said later on, cannot be regarded as representing or impersonating Ogun; he *is* Ogun, his own consciousness temporarily wiped out. In another drama, *The Bacchae of Euripides* (London, 1973), which is an adaptation of a classical Greek drama, Soyinka stresses the similarities between Ogun and the Greek god Dionysus to such an extent that they appear to be almost identical.

Most frequently, Ogun works through human agents, let us call them 'men of Ogun'. In this category we find some of the characters in Soyinka's dramas, namely Igwezu in

The Swamp Dwellers (in *Three Plays*, Ibadan, 1963), Eman in *The Strong Breed* (in *Three Plays*, Ibadan, 1963), Demoke in *A Dance of the Forests*, Daodu in *Kongi's Harvest* (London, Ibadan, Nairobi, 1967), Isola in *Camwood on the Leaves* (London, 1973), and Olunde in *Death and the King's Horseman* (London, 1975). As 'men of Ogun' we may also regard the persona in 'Idanre', and Sekoni and Ofeyi, who appear in the novels *The Interpreters* (London, 1965) and *Season of Anomy* (London, 1973) respectively.

In some works, we find human representatives of Obatala, the Yoruba god of peace, order and harmony, acting together with the 'men of Ogun'. Examples of characters of this kind are the blind beggar in *The Swamp Dwellers* and Bandele in *The Interpreters*. In the following, I shall concentrate on *The Swamp Dwellers*, *A Dance of the Forests*, *The Road*, *The Bacchae of Euripides*, *Idanre and Other Poems*, and *The Interpreters*.

The Swamp Dwellers, probably Soyinka's earliest play, concerns a conflict between the young Igwezu and the priest, the Kadiye, of his native village. Igwezu, having unsuccessfully sought his fortune in the city, returns to his native village to find his harvest destroyed by a flood, in spite of his having sacrificed to the village deity, the so-called 'Serpent of the Swamps', before leaving. In his bitter disappointment, Igwezu attacks the Kadiye with bitter rancour, accusing him of feathering his own nest at the expense of the villagers. After this unprecedented insult to the most sacred person in the village, Igwezu has no choice but to leave again, this time for good. The climax of this drama is a scene where Igwezu, temporarily standing in for his father Makuri, the village barber, shaves the Kadiye. In this scene, Igwezu accuses and insults the Kadiye, while the sharp razor in his hand seems less and less like an innocent tool of trade, more and more like a dangerous weapon. Igwezu, then, performs his act of rebellion while acting as a barber, a member of a professional group protected by Ogun and holding in his hand a razor, sacred to Ogun like all metal tools. We may also observe that Igwezu's defiance puts him in a situation characterized by both anguish and physical danger. The anguish is the anguish of absolute loneliness and alienation, for Igwezu's behaviour towards the Kadiye makes him forever an outcast from his native village. Where the physical danger is concerned, we are informed that Igwezu must leave the village quickly, before the people start calling for blood.[2] Now, as Soyinka interprets the myth of Ogun, e.g. in his essay 'The Fourth Stage' (in *Myth, Literature and the African World*, Cambridge, 1976), the pioneer god experienced both pain, anguish and mortal danger as he bridged the gulf between gods and humans, between the actual and the possible. To my mind, Ogun's presence can be clearly felt in *The Swamp Dwellers*, in spite of the fact that he is never mentioned by name.

The same can be said of Obatala, represented in this drama by a blind beggar who arrives in Igwezu's native village hoping to transform part of the swamp near the village into cultivable land. However, he is told that it would be sacrilege to do such a thing, as the swamp is sacred to 'the Serpent of the Swamps'. According to Yoruba mythology, earth was once nothing but a big swamp. It was Obatala who gave earth its present appearance, by transforming this swamp into cultivable land. Now, this is exactly what the beggar, too, hopes to achieve - making marshy ground arable. It is believed that Obatala cannot exert his creative influence until after Ogun's heroic act of self-sacrifice. In a similar manner, the beggar stays on to cultivate the land, after Igwezu has left. Obatala stands for peace and harmony, which are also distinguishing features of the beggar's personality, in spite of all the sufferings and bitter disappointments he has had to go through in his life. There are other signs of a connection between the beggar and Obatala. The beggar is blind, and the blind are sacred to Obatala. Furthermore, the beggar is dressed in white, which is Obatala's colour, symbolizing 'holiness' and purity.

A Dance of the Forests was first produced in Lagos in 1960, in connection with Nigeria's official celebration of her independence. In this drama, we see a great many people gathered in celebration of a very important national festival, to which they have also invited the spirits of illustrious ancestors. However, the ancestors sent by the gods fall far short of the expectations of the humans. What they wished for were warriors, conquerors, empire builders, philosophers, mystics and so on, but what they finally get are two poor, restless spirits, who, while they still belonged to the world of the living, received extremely cruel and unjust treatment at the hands of a megalomaniac tyrant from the so-called 'glorious past' of the nation. What the gods want the humans to realize is that their history is nothing but a cycle of senseless cruelty, and that their only chance to survive is to be aware of, and prepared to learn from, the terrible and tragic mistakes of earlier generations. Among the gods, Ogun is the one most eager to liberate the humans from the doom of meaningless repetition. Ogun's representative among the humans is Demoke, the wood-carver. Demoke has been commissioned by the village council to carve a totem for the national festival. This totem turns out quite differently from what the council expects, for one of Demoke's most important sources of inspiration is the cruel, profoundly immoral queen, Madame Tortoise, one of the most reprehensible characters in the history of the nation. What Demoke wants is to remind his fellow humans that their past has been far from great and beautiful, thus giving them the opportunity to avoid repeating the mistakes and cruelties of earlier generations. Demoke wants to help others to lead better lives, but he can achieve this only after deliberately killing his apprentice Oremole, who is a follower of Eshuoro, the humans' bitterest and most dangerous enemy among the gods. Demoke's creativity, like that of Ogun, is, then, closely linked with sudden death. This rich and difficult drama ends on a note of very guarded optimism. Ogun's final victory is far from certain, for he has many powerful enemies, and man's worst enemy, now as ever, is man himself.

In the drama *The Road*, first produced in London in 1965, we meet a group of people - lorry-drivers, policemen and others - who live near a motor road somewhere in Nigeria. The principal character, Professor, is the owner of a small shop, where he sells parts of wrecked cars to drivers in need of spare parts. Professor is a complicated character, full of seeming contradictions. He is a criminal, a liar and a cheat - he is a forger of driver's licences and similar documents, and he is not above actually causing accidents whenever his supply of spare parts needs refilling. However, he is also deeply concerned with spiritual matters. With the tenacity of a man possessed, he searches for the key to a mysterious truth, which he calls 'the Word', and which he believes to be closely related to death. In Professor's opinion, whoever does not understand the meaning of death, cannot understand the meaning of life; it is probably this conviction of his that has caused him to make his home so close to the road, where death is never far away.

The road is the central symbol of this drama. It symbolizes both Ogun and that cosmic abyss, which he was the first to bridge. The road, like Ogun, is closely linked to both life and death, for it provides a livelihood for the lorry-drivers, but as soon as they set off on one of their transport missions, it threatens to kill them. However, Ogun is present in this play not only in the road itself, but also in the person of Murano, the mute.

Concerning Murano, we are informed that he has been run down by a lorry while performing a ritual dance in honour of Ogun. During this dance, he was completely possessed by the god, his own individuality temporarily obliterated. In the accident, Murano is hurt so badly that he cannot return to life, but he does not actually die. He is stranded in a spiritual 'no-man's-land' between life and death, filled with the spirit of Ogun, sharing in the god's profound knowledge of the nature of being, but unable to pass this knowledge on to others, since he is a mute. Professor finds the wounded Murano, tends him and studies him closely in the hope of finding the truth by using Ogun, part of whom is imprisoned in Murano's body. But Professor is not successful. Not until he himself lies dying by the roadside, stabbed to death by a gangster, can he partake of the knowledge he has been searching for; only then are the secrets of death – and life – revealed to him. Professor can be said to arrive at the ultimate knowledge through the agency of Ogun, for when Professor leaves this world for the great unknown, he does so as a result of being stabbed with a knife, and knives, like all metal tools, are sacred to Ogun.

The Bacchae of Euripides, first performed in London in 1973, can be regarded as a special instance of the presence of Ogun in the dramas of Soyinka. In this work, we see Dionysus liberating the city of Thebes from oppression and terror by causing the death of the young tyrant Pentheus, who is torn to pieces by his own mother, Agave, and her sisters, while they are in a state of bacchanalian frenzy. Dionysus, like Ogun, is a both cruel and benevolent god, who renews and heals, but who can also break and destroy, a god whose goal is life, but whose means are sometimes death. Soyinka introduces several Yoruba elements in his version of the Euripidean drama and, as mentioned earlier, stresses the similarity between Dionysus and Ogun to such a degree that they occasionally seem identical rather than closely related. For instance, the leader of the slaves of Thebes, who is an African, invokes Dionysus in words very much similar to those used in certain traditional Yoruba songs in honour of Ogun.

In the poem 'Idanre', Soyinka retells the myth of how Ogun massacred his own soldiers. When the god comes to his senses and realizes what he has done, his sorrow is so deep that, to begin with, it seems quite inconsolable. He has made a fatal mistake – he has failed to observe the individual, the particular, that which separates one human being from another, ally from enemy. This oversight has resulted in an orgy of senseless slaughter. The truth so painfully revealed to Ogun can be put like this: where the individual does not exist, or is not recognized, there is nothing but death, the absolute, definitive death which, far from being a precondition of life, is its exact opposite. A human race composed of people with no individuality of their own is like a flock of sheep being led to the slaughter; they live and die without understanding why. On the other hand, a human race composed of true individuals will sometimes produce people who are radically different from all others, who are prepared to sacrifice everything to discover the truth about life, later to share this knowledge with their fellow mortals. Not until the humans have seen the truth, and understood the interplay of life and death, can they live fully and completely. Consequently, the presence of exceptional individuals can be regarded as a precondition of life, if by life we mean something other and greater than a merely vegetative existence.

Ogun himself is an exceptional individual – he dared what none of the other gods dared when he cleared a road between them and the humans – but not until this day of slaughter does he become fully aware of this. Now that he has realized the importance of individualism, he immediately takes it upon him to share his vitally important knowledge with mankind. He will teach us to fire not one big, collective kiln, but a large number of kilns, one for each person, and he will make us rightfully proud of what is produced by each of these kilns, the symbols of individual creativity. 'Idanre' ends with a homage to Ogun, the one who, in his complex personality, unites all apparent opposites, the one who both creates and destroys.

The novel *The Interpreters* is about a group of young Nigerian intellectuals who are trying to come to terms with life in a modern African state. Among them, there is a true 'man of Ogun', namely the engineer Sekoni, member of a professional group under the protection of Ogun. Sekoni tries in every way to use his knowledge for the good of his people, but is hindered and eventually confined in a mental hospital by stupid and corrupt politicians and officials. After his discharge, he gives up engineering to take up wood-carving, another profession under the protection of Ogun. In his wooden sculptures, Sekoni tries to express his belief that the universe is an almost inconceivably great unity, within which everything – now and then, the living, the dead and the unborn – exists simultaneously. To Sekoni, progress is not wiping out the memory of the past and marching through the present towards the future, all the time staring forward. To his way of thinking, progress is possible only to those who understand the coexistence of everything and who are able to reconcile a respect for ancient tradition with the will to change and improve their society. After Sekoni has been killed in a road accident, his closest friends, under the discreet guidance of Bandele, the 'man of Obatala', develop in such a way that they, too, become more and more deserving of the epithet 'men of Ogun'.

When discussing Yoruba mythology in the works of Soyinka, it is important to remember that he never uses myths for their own sake. His main object is to draw attention to present conditions, using myths to make clear the hidden patterns of the here and now. In *The Swamp Dwellers*, Igwezu, the 'man of Ogun', attempts to rid his village of anti-progressive traditions; in *A Dance of the Forests*, Ogun and his servant Demoke attempt to make people aware of the fact that their ideas of the glorious past are without any foundation in truth, in order that they might learn from history's mistakes; in *The Road*, Ogun, without actually showing himself, strikes down the corrupt and dishonest; in *The Bacchae of Euripides*, the

'Ogun-ized' Dionysus brings about the downfall of a cruel tyrant; in 'Idanre', Ogun and the persona of the poem sing the praises of individualism; in *The Interpreters*, the main characters attempt to do away with the greed, falsehood and corruption that dominate the society in which they live.

To Soyinka, the mythical figures represent a positive attitude to life, a sort of optimism in spite of everything. This is apparent from his treatment of them in his darkest, most pessimistic works, namely those conceived during his imprisonment 1967-69, in the crushing shadow of the Nigerian civil war. Besides a book of prison reminiscences entitled *The Man Died* (London, 1972), these works are the drama *Madmen and Specialists* (London, 1971), the volume of poetry *A Shuttle in the Crypt* (London, 1972), and the novel *Season of Anomy*. The principal character of *Madmen and Specialists*, a surgeon by the name of Bero, is a potential 'man of Ogun' who fails in his duty in a most disgraceful manner by acting as medical adviser and chief torturer for the totalitarian government of his country; in *A Shuttle in the Crypt*, the gods are so far removed from the human field of vision as to be hardly discernible; in *Season of Anomy*, which describes life in an African state under a totalitarian government of the most brutal sort, the servants of Ogun do not proceed to action until the final chapter.

Soyinka is writing in a period of cultural transition. The African society mirrored in his works is characterized by conflicts between ancient and modern, native and foreign, and between rebellious individuals and the establishment; conflicts that lead to swift and radical changes, which Soyinka seems to regard as earthly counterparts of the universal transformation which resulted from Ogun's mighty leap across what Soyinka frequently refers to as 'the abyss of transition'.[3]

Soyinka's 'men of Ogun' offer no definitive solutions to the social, historical and metaphysical problems with which they wrestle – they merely make solutions possible. What the author wants to say by this is that it is possible to find positive solutions to the problems dealt with in his texts, but that the prerequisite for this to happen is the presence of strong, self-dependent and tenacious individuals who dare 'clear a path' for the less enterprising majority. Still, not even the existence of such individuals is a guarantee for a better future – they merely make it possible. Within the framework of Soyinka's writings, Ogun and his followers can be said to represent an optimistic view of the future – but the optimism is always very guarded.

NOTES

1. Daryll Forde, *The Yoruba-Speaking Peoples of South-Western Nigeria* (London, 1951), p. 29. J.D.Y. Peel, *Aladura, A Religious Movement Among the Yoruba* (London, 1968), p. 30. William Bascom, *The Yoruba of South-western Nigeria* (New York, 1969), p. 77.
2. Wole Soyinka, *Three Plays* (Ibadan, 1963), p. 42.
3. Wole Soyinka, *Myth, Literature and the African World*, pp. 26, 29, 31, 32, 58, 140-60.

African Traditional Theatre and Its Influence on Modern Drama

KACKE GÖTRICK

When analysing the modern African drama it is common-place to make comparisons with Western drama, and such comparisons are also often relevant. Early critics of African drama completely neglected the African theatrical back-ground. Gradually, however, the Western critics, aided by their African colleagues, have come to realize firstly, that Africa has theatrical traditions of its own, and secondly, that modern playwrights make use of these traditions. But since our knowledge of these traditions is still fragmentary, there is much room for impressionism.

Many critics have maintained that modern dramas by Yoruba playwrights are influenced by traditional theatre or ritual. At times a specific source has been mentioned. But more often no such source has been indicated, and some-times this seems to be due to an inclination on the part of Western critics to attribute anything that they do not im-mediately understand to the traditional background of the author.

Many Western critics thus seem unaware of their own basic assumption that the African writers are not truly original but only imitating Western theatre and/or African traditional theatre.

When it comes to the African writers' use of their own traditional theatre, research has only begun seriously to explore this topic. There are many problems involved, for instance our fragmentary knowledge of the traditions. And, linked to this, there is our ethnocentric definition of 'drama' and 'theatre'.

Access to primary source material also constitutes a problem: only a few first-hand descriptions of traditional theatre exist, and some of them are hard to come by. Moreover, the theatrical activities also are not so easily accessible. And of course, a major problem is that it is difficult for an outsider to achieve an understanding of cultures so different from his or her own.

These problems can be solved only gradually. While solving them it is most important, however, that we are aware of the problems involved in working with different world-views. Impressionism creeps in when we interpret another world-view as if it were our own, i.e. we use the knowledge acquired within our own culture as a means of interpretation also when it comes to contexts where this knowledge is not applicable.

One possible method to circumvent impressionism is to use structuralism. Although insensitive to nuances, a structural method can help in sorting a seemingly chaotic material into a manageable initial model of understanding. And this was the line I took in my book *Apidan Theatre and Modern Drama*, investigating the influence of the Igungun Apidan theatre on the modern drama by Yoruba playwrights.[1]

Although the culture of the Yoruba people in Nigeria is one of the best known in West Africa, it is still difficult to arrive at a close-up of their theatrical traditions and their meanings. With written sources on one of these traditions, the Apidan theatre, covering the period from 1826 to 1982, and a number of live performances by different troupes in the area of Oyo-Ibadan-Ilaro in Western Nigeria as material, the following description was made.

A performance is made up of a varying number of entities, each entity being a completed whole, which need not presuppose the preceding entity as far as the story line is concerned. This fact allows the entities to be interchangeable.

Each entity - drama - belongs to one of the genres *idan* or *efe* or *transition from idan to efe*. The genres are differentiated not so much by properties inherent in the dramas as such, as by their relation to the surrounding reality. It is, then, the audience's attributing the entity to fiction or to non-fiction that determines the genre. And so one specific drama may belong to different genres, depending on the context and the audience.

A performance always starts with an address to the forefathers and the powers that rule the universe, to obtain a blessing so that no harm may be done to the performance. There is also an address to the audience.

In a *Dance* contact is made with superhuman powers, and this contact is demonstrated by the *Acrobatics* following. The *Dance* and the *Acrobatics* are not fictional, contain no role-playing, and belong to the idan genre.

A following *Mat Dance* simultaneously performs a miracle - the mat seems to move by itself - and imitates a feat, performed in another theatre tradition. Thus non-fiction and fiction blend, and the drama belongs to the transitional genre. The *Mat Dance* may be followed by another drama of the same genre.

A number of dramas belonging to the efe genre follow, such as *Drunkard*, *Ijesa Man*, and *The Pig*. All clearly imitate the title figure and illustrate a state of affairs, rather than narrating a story or acting out a conflict.

All performances end with *The Beautiful Bride*, where the male troupe leader excels in female dancing, thus bringing opposite qualities together in harmony.

There is a little dialogue or text. Music, mask, costume and dance are the main elements. As to the genres, a performance is always made up according to a set order. The performance starts with idan dramas. Then comes a transition from idan to efe, and finally one or several efe dramas. A performance seen by Clapperton and Lander in 1826 ended after this. But nowadays this sequence is repeated, and a performance may comprise several such sequences.

What marks the difference between an Apidan performance and a Western theatre performance of today is the relation between fiction and non-fiction. Whereas Western theatre is all fictional, the Apidan theatre contains a blend of fiction and reality, so that idan entities are meant to be religiously efficacious. They are performed to give a result far beyond the theatrical event. They are taken to imply a communication not only between actors and audience but also between actors and audience on the one hand and superhuman powers on the other. The idan dramas address these powers. In the transitional dramas knowledge gained from the communication with the supernatural powers is brought back to the human audience. And in the efe dramas, addressing the human audience, this knowledge is made use of to expose the vices in society. The educative function is, then, very pronounced in the Apidan theatre.

It is the interchangeability of the dramas and the communication with superhuman powers in particular which pose problems when a modern playwright wants to use the Apidan theatre as a model for a modern drama.

A comparison between a great number of modern anglophone dramas by Yoruba writers and the sequential structure of the Apidan theatre shows that three types of influence can be found, depending on the complexity of the transformed Apidan structure.

The simplest transformed structure is individual elements like music and story-telling. Ola Rotimi's drama *Ovonramwen Nogbaisi*[2] provides a good example. In the beginning of the drama, music is played as it would have been played in real life in circumstances similar to those portrayed. In other words, the music is mimetic. With the peripeteia, however, the music takes on functions shared with the Apidan theatre, namely to comment on the characters and to intervene in their actions. The music ceases to be mimetic and becomes an actor or agent of its own.

A more complex transformed structure is an individual Apidan drama that has either been used as a point of departure for an entire modern drama, or for a scene or part of a scene in a modern drama. In Rotimi's drama *Kurunmi*[3] we find an example of the Apidan drama *Oyinbo* (White Man) being transformed into a character, namely that of Reverend Mann. *Oyinbo* is also transformed into a specific scene, namely that between Field Marshal Kurunmi and Mann. This scene ends in the two sitting opposite each other croaking like frogs. Like the Apidan *Oyinbo*, the character Mann and this frog scene portray the white man as an alien, as somebody who is unable to understand the Yoruba way of thinking. Even the way the frog scene is placed in the overall structure of *Kurunmi* is equivalent to the position *Oyinbo* would have in an Apidan performance.

The highest complexity of the transformed Apidan structure is found where the entire structuring principle of an Apidan performance guides the structuring of an entire modern play. Sanya Dosunmu's *God's Deputy*[4] is an example. On the level of the content the drama imitates a religiously efficacious activity. This can be seen as an attempt to give the audience a sensation similar to that created by an idan drama of the Apidan theatre. Where knowledge given by the god to his deputy, the King, is shared by the people of the drama, the audience may see a kind of correspondence to the transitional phase of an Apidan sequence. Some of the scenes of the drama could be exchanged for a new choreography or another game, a fact that brings the interchangeability of the Apidan theatre to mind. The end of *God's Deputy* is very similar to the last drama of any Apidan performance, *The Beautiful Bride*. Even the bridal procession out off the stage is there.

Although this structural method does reveal examples of influence on anglophone dramas by a traditional Yoruba theatre, the influence is not found to be as frequent as some Western critics want us to believe. However, a different method might arrive at a different result. By analysing much more sophisticated levels of meaning, Yoruba scholars like Femi Osofisan have argued that such different kinds of performance as ritual theatre and Wole Soyinka's dramas express common ideas generated by the same Yoruba world-view.[5] Such a method demands deep insights into the Yoruba culture, its religion and philosophy, ethics and aesthetics, such as few Western critics have mustered.

NOTES

1. Kacke Götrick, *Apidan Theatre and Modern Drama* (Stockholm, 1984).
2. Ola Rotimi, *Ovonramwen Nogbaisi, an historical tragedy in English* (Benin City and Ibadan, 1974).
3. Ola Ratimi, *Kurunmi - an Historical tragedy* (Ibadan, 1971).
4. Sanya Dosunmu, *God's Deputy*, in Cosmo Pieterse, ed., *Short African Plays* (London, 1972).
5. Femi Osofisan, 'The origin of drama in West Africa: a study of the development of drama from the traditional forms to modern theatre in English and French' (Ph.D. dissertation, University of Ibadan, 1973).

On Writing *Slave Song* *

DAVID DABYDEEN

In describing the plantation experience which is a dominant feature of the West Indies, the white English poets falsified that experience through their peculiar use of the English language. James Grainger, for example, published in the eighteenth century *The Sugar Cane*, in which the barbaric experience of slavery is wrapped in a napkin of poetic diction and converted into civilized expression. Grainger did not speak of 'overseer', he used instead the poetic pastoral term 'master-swain'; he wrote of 'assistant planters' instead of 'slaves', and 'Afric's sable progeny' instead of 'blacks'. *The Sugar Cane* is an excellent example in English verse of the refusal to call a spade a spade. Coleridge, whilst an undergraduate at Cambridge, wrote his first major poem (for which he won the university's Gold Medal, metal which probably came from the colonised regions of El Dorado), which was a Greek ode on the slave trade. Coleridge exercised his erudition, and the black experience was contained within the elegant boundaries of civilized language.

I write on plantation life in Creole, in reaction against this tradition (one always writes in response to English poetry), emphasizing the barbaric energy and brokenness of Creole.

In the introduction to *Slave Song*, I attempt to go into the linguistics or technicalities of the language and I focus on

53

what I call the vulgarity of the language; 'vulgarity' in the classical sense of what is native and local but also what tends towards the obscene. I say about the vulgarity of the language that it is the vulgarity of the people – and here I am talking about the canecutters in Berbice in Guyana. It is the vulgarity of the people's way of life. There is little grace, peace or politeness in their lives, only a lot of cane. If cane dominates life, it also dominates death; if a Guyanese peasant dies, and one enquires about the cause of his death, the invariable answer is 'sugar in the blood', meaning diabetes. You could be dying of a heart attack or coronary thrombosis or cancer, but the common explanation is that you are dying of 'sugar in the blood'. Cane sugar dominates death itself. The language is angry, crude, energetic. The canecutter chopping away at the crops bursts into a spate of obscene words, a natural gush from the gut, like fresh faeces. It is hard to put two words together in Creole without swearing. Words are spat out from the mouth like live squibs, not pronounced with elocution. English diction is cut up and this adds to the abruptness of the language.

I also go on to talk about the tragic potential of the language. Another feature of the language is its brokenness, no doubt reflecting the brokenness and suffering of its original users, African slaves and East Indian indentured labourers. Its potential as a naturally tragic language is there in the brokenness and rawness, which is like the rawness of a wound. If one has learnt and used Queen's English for a long time, the return into Creole is painful, almost nauseous, for the language is uncomfortably raw. One has to shed one's protective sheath of abstracts and let the tongue move freely and bleed again. One has to get accustomed to the unsheathing of the tongue and the contact of raw matter. I am interested in the tension between the barbaric, broken, harsh language and the expression of something beautiful; the tension of having to express something beautiful in a language that belongs to the mud. I wanted to show in *Slave Song* the Creole mind struggling and straining after concepts of beauty and purity but held back by its physically crude vocabulary. The canecutter aspires to the lyrical experience and expression but cannot escape his condition of squalor nor the crude diction that such a condition generates. So, to describe beauty, he struggles to transform vulgar words and concepts into lyrical ones, the result being poignant and tragic. He has no poetical words because his experience of life under colonial rule was never poetical. The cry for transfiguration or abstraction is constantly frustrated; he cannot escape his words, cannot escape the mud.

The challenge of writing in Creole then is, paradoxically, similar to the purpose of Grainger and Coleridge in that what I am attempting to do is to convert barbarism into a dream of romance. The poems I write are really about dreams because the poems retreat consciously from the real world of sado-masochism. By sado-masochism I mean the world of the colonial canecutter and overseer but I also mean the contemporary world of Blacks in Britain. You know that England has been described as 'the last colony of the British Empire' in that you have the same energizing myths about black people in England that prevailed in the colonies, the confrontation and the violence between Blacks and Whites in contemporary Britain. It is a reflection of that historical phenomenon in the Caribbean. So while I talk of the real world of sado-masochism and my poetry retreating from that world, I just do not mean the colonial but also the contemporary world. But I also mean the White British world of televisual commerce, a world of instant glamour, instant violence, Americanism and what I also call the world of journalistic prose which is a measure of all that instant Americanism. And one retreats from that world and attempts to recreate imaginatively images of a new romance (when you retreat from the real world, you can only live in a world of images).

The idea of originality is a Caribbean obsession. Wilson

Harris is obsessed with notions of originality, the theme of reversing, or remaking, or transcending history, what he calls 'mending the broken conceptions of history'; if you like, redressing rape. In the introduction to *Slave Song*, I call this 'the cry for transfiguration', the movement away from darkness to light.

In my own writing, Hindu concerns with purification and rebirth, which are part of my ancestral Hindu set of beliefs, are absorbed into the larger Caribbean obsession with cleansing and new beginnings. One could therefore say that Caribbean writers, as exemplified in Wilson Harris, are involved in a process of alchemy, trying to convert base metal into gold, even the mythical gold of El Dorado. The Caribbean artist is primarily an alchemist. This is not peculiar to the Caribbean. One finds the same literally as well as metaphorically in the works of Strindberg. But in so far as we always had this historic desire to cleanse ourselves of history, we found that we could only do that through the recreation of dream images and of original myth.

The attempt at revising history imaginatively involves too the renewal or purification of conventional English imagery. The attempt at purification is not just a notional one but also stylistic and formal. For example, in English romantic verse, the moon is associated with private love, and the sun with public intrusion and rude disturbance of romance. These are conventions that over the centuries have become stale and tedious. In my own romantic poetry I consciously take on this apparatus of clichéd images but attempt to infuse it with our ancestral experience so that, because of the tropical experience of cane cutting, the sun becomes associated with public (or communal) labour and brutality, and with the white overseer. And the moon is associated with the fantasy of sleep, of rest, and in particular, the secret fantasy of sleep with the white woman. Another example: if you read Spenser or Sidney, or the Silver Poets of the sixteenth century, you will find a profusion of images about slavery employed in describing love. Spenser is always kneeling at the foot of his Lady, or else she has her heel at his neck, or else he is transfixed by her gaze, or else enchained by her cruelty. Such images of bondage are images of sado-masochism and underclothing excitement. In my poetry, I take on this apparatus of slavery but with purified purpose.

Of course I write poetry in English as well as in Creole, depending on the level of abstraction that I am struggling for. Creole can operate brilliantly in terms of images and symbols, and in the exploitation of certain rhythms that are local and native, but, as with all languages, there are limitations of expression. I find that English has a flexibility as well as enormous limitations. I cannot achieve the same choreography in English as I can in Creole. I cannot achieve the same level of abstraction in Creole that I can in English.

---

*) *Slave Song* (Dangaroo Press, 1984) was winner of the 1984 Commonwealth Poetry Prize.

David Dabydeen

THE SEXUAL WORD

She dreaded the naïvety
Of longing for rebirth,
Beheld him stuttering out his dream
Of journeys ended:
The howling oceanic thrust of history
That heaved forth savages in strange canoes
Weighed with magical cannon and muzzle and anklechain
Stilled
To a pool in his eye
Through which he saw
The solitary quay,
The new seed.

He burnt his mind in acid of his own alchemy
Urging song from his hurt mouth
Desperate to colonize her
In images of gold and fertility
To remake her from his famished rib
To redeem her from the white world
That would reduce him to mute captivity.

She refused the embrace of fantasy,
Unable to be torn up, transplanted,
Stripped, raped, broken and made to bear

Beautiful bastard fruit –
She could not endure the repetition
Necessary for new beginning

Yet was ravished by the poetry.

COOLIE WOMAN

Jasmattie live in bruk –
Down hut big like Bata shoe-box,
Beat clothes, weed yard, chop wood, feed fowl
For this body and that body and every blasted body,
Fetch water, all day fetch water like if the whole –
Whole slow-flowing Canje river God create
Just for *she* one own bucket.

Till she foot-bottom crack and she hand cut-up
And curse swarm from the mouth like red-ants
And she cough blood on the ground but mash it in:
Because Jasmattie heart hard, she mind set hard

To hustle save she one-one slow penny
Because one-one dutty mek dam cross the Canje
And she son Harilall *got* to go school in Georgetown,
Must wear clean starch pants, or they go laugh at he,
Strap leather on he foot, and he *must* read book,
Learn talk proper, tek exam, go to England university,
Not turn out like he rum-sucker chamar dadee.

* dutty: piece of earth
* chamar: low-caste coolie

THE TOILET ATTENDANT WRITES HOME

Taana boy, how you do?
How Shanti stay? An Sukhoo?
Mosquito still a-bite all-you?
Juncha dead true-true?
Mala bruk-foot set?
Food deh foh eat yet?

England nice, snow an dem ting,
A land deh say fit for a king,
Iceapple plenty on de tree an bird a-sing-
Is de beginning of wha deh call 'The Spring'.

An I eating enough for all a-we
An reading book bad – bad.

But is wha mek Matam wife fall sick
An Sonnel cow suck dry wid tick?

Soon, I go turn lawya or dacta,
But, just now, passage money run out
So I tek lil wuk –
I is a Deputy Sanitary Inspecta,
Big – big office boy! Tie round me neck!
Brand new uniform, one big bunch keys!
If Ma can see me now how she go please......

Bilat

PRAFULLA MOHANTI

I did not think the sun could shine so brightly in England.

It was a July morning in 1960. The P & O ship had anchored sometime during the previous night. When I woke up the ship was still. I realized we had arrived at Tilbury. I opened the porthole and saw hundreds of seagulls flying around. The water was muddy but the sun was glistening on it.

I ran to the upper deck. The sky was blue and the air fresh. I felt excited. I was in a new country, the country of my dreams. I had come to England for further qualifications and experience after graduating as an architect from Bombay University.

England was known as 'Bilayat' in Hindi. A Bilayati qualification was highly regarded in India. Everything Bilayati was considered superior to anything 'Deshi' (Indian). When I was studying architecture in Bombay most of my teachers had been educated in England. The students thought they were more important than the teachers with Indian qualifications. We were told that English architecture was the best. Architects with British qualifications were respected and got better jobs and commissions.

I heard the word 'Bilat', the Oriya equivalent of 'Bilayat', for the first time in my childhood in Nanpur, my village in Orissa. The village was totally isolated and I was not conscious of a world outside. When I was five years old my mother consulted the astrologer about my future. He was an old man with white hair and a long beard. Peering through a pair of steel-framed spectacles he carefully studied my jatak (horoscope), inscribed on a palm leaf. He drew diagrams on the mud floor with a piece of clay chalk and declared solemnly, 'This boy will go to Bilat.'

I was intrigued. I had heard names like 'Kalikata' and 'Kataka', where some of the villagers worked, but 'Bilat' was a totally new word.

As soon as the astrologer left I asked my mother what 'Bilat' meant. She told me it was the country where the Gora Sahibs lived. They were the Rajas of India.

'How do you get there?'

'By boat. There are seven seas to cross.'

It seemed a long way away.

'What language do they speak?'

'"Angrezi".'

'Would you like me to go to Bilat?'

She smiled. 'No. I don't want you to go anywhere. Those who go to Bilat lose their caste. They eat beef and drink alcohol. But I've heard that a boy from a poor family in Cuttack went to Bilat to study. He has come back and got a big job. But he didn't eat any beef.'

'So why don't you want me to go to Bilat? I promise not to eat beef or drink alcohol.'

'Where is the money? You must study well here. My only wish is for God to give you a long life.'

'Would you mind if I went to Bilat?'

She stroked my head. 'It is a different world.'

If I want to go to Bilat, I told myself, I must learn to read and write in English. There was a Brahmin in the village who sold books, papers, and writing materials from his house. I went to him and bought a book on how to teach myself English.

I asked my sister to help me. I told her, 'The astrologer says I'll go to Bilat.'

'But he also said the same thing to me,' she replied. 'He always says absurd things to please his jezmans (clients).'

I did not know then that my grandmother had forbidden her to go to school when she reached puberty. She was afraid my sister might become a 'Kirastani' (Christian).

In the years that followed I had forgotten the astrologer's forecast. I suddenly realized it had come true.

The Immigration Officer was polite. 'I hope you will be as happy in my country as I was in yours.'

I was in Bilat.

From Tilbury I came to Liverpool Street by train. Everything looked so clean. The trains in India were always crowded and the passengers had to fight to get into them. The seats were so dusty that they had to be wiped before sitting down. Here the seats were upholstered and travel seemed simple.

The excitement of arriving in a new country was overwhelming. I was so involved in my own thoughts that I was not aware of the other passengers or the view through the window.

When the train pulled into Liverpool Street station, the architecture reminded me of the Victoria Terminus in Bombay. But the atmosphere was quiet and orderly without crowds of coolies waiting to invade the compartments and haggle over the transport of baggage. Instead of brown faces there were white faces everywhere.

I was relieved to see Tom, who had been waiting for me on the platform. He was the only person I knew in England. He was a few years older than me and I had met him in Bombay where he was working for a British company. I had brought my three gods with me – small painted wooden figures of Lord Jagannath, an incarnation of Vishnu, his brother Balabhadra, and their sister Subhadra. They were my friends and protectors. I prayed and talked to them every day.

I climbed down from the train clutching my gods in one hand and my suitcase in the other. In my shoulder bag which I always carried with me were my painting and drawing materials – sketch pads, brushes, and paints.

Tom greeted me. 'Welcome to London.' He lived at Surbiton and we went there by taxi. To my surprise the buildings of central London resembled parts of Bombay. I had read so much about the River Thames that when Tom pointed it out to me I was terribly disappointed. It looked like an Indian canal. I was used to wide rivers with banks of clean white sand. The houses in the suburbs with their tiled roofs and neat little gardens seemed to continue for ever. After a while I was unable to distinguish one from the other.

Groups of people were sunbathing in the parks; half-naked young men and women kissed and cuddled. It was a strange experience for me. In India people always hide from the sun and there is no free mixing between boys and girls; kissing is even forbidden on the cinema screen.

Tom lived in a 1930s purpose-built block of flats overlooking a large private garden. When we arrived, his mother was waiting for us. I greeted her saying 'Namaste', joining my hands together as in prayer. Then we shook hands and she kissed me on the cheek, enquiring whether my journey had been comfortable. She had cooked a large meal specially for me, lamb curry and rice, English style. She was in her fifties and a widow. Her husband died when Tom was a small boy, but she did not marry again. She lived by herself in a small town in Sussex and from time to time came to London to stay with her son.

I gave her a handwoven silk stole I had brought from Orissa. It is an Indian custom to carry presents for the host. She examined it carefully, wrapped it round her shoulders, and went to look at herself in the mirror. She came back, kissed me again, and said 'Thank you'.

I looked forward to my first Christmas in England with great anticipation. Around November the atmosphere changed and the shops started displaying special Christmas goods and decorations. The main shopping streets were illuminated at night.

Tom and his mother brought out their address books and prepared lists of friends and relatives. 'Christmas is the time to remember friends and relatives and send them cards,' they told me. They bought their cards but I drew mine. I thought it was more personal and my list was short.

In India there is a religious festival practically every month. My village school closed for several days at Christmas. We called it 'Xmas holiday' but did not know what it meant. For the autumn festival of Dassera my father came on a long holiday with presents for me. There was a great sense of participation in the village and my mother prepared many kinds of cakes which we ate and distributed among our friends.

I was disappointed when I was told that my office would close for only two days, but I noticed my colleagues taking time off to do their Christmas shopping. A secretary told me she had been buying her presents since the previous Christmas and had even kept some which were given to her. I noticed that the closeness of the relationship was measured by the price of the presents. There seemed little religious significance, but the shopkeepers were happy.

Christmas also meant party time. I did not like parties in England. Guests stood in little groups clutching their wine glasses, gossiping with their friends, and ignoring the others. But the office Christmas party seemed different. We all joined in, there was plenty to drink, and everybody was friendly. I was also invited to other office parties. In the week before Christmas there were two or three every night. It was a time to be nice to everybody, but after Christmas the smiling faces became gloomy again.

I liked the habit of giving presents; it was very Indian. I bought several small packets of the best Darjeeling tea available in London to give to my friends. I gave a packet to a colleague in the office. She was very pleased and said it would go with the Christmas cake. After Christmas she came up to me and said, 'Prafulla, we enjoyed your tea very much, but it blocked up my sink.' I had forgotten to warn her that the tea had large leaves.

On Christmas Day I woke up in the morning to find a stocking on my bed, full of little presents. Tom's mother said Father Christmas must have left them.

We had spent many hours the previous day decorating the flat. In one corner of the living room we placed the Christmas tree with all its ornaments – light bulbs, stars, and an angel. Attractively wrapped parcels were piled round its base. We hung Christmas cards on strings and put them round the room. Tom's relatives started arriving at eleven, one by one, carrying presents in their arms. The flat vibrated with greetings: 'Happy Christmas'; 'Happy New Year.'

The table was laid with the best china and the family silver. Tom was very particular about the drinks and had bought champagne, sherry, wine, whisky, gin, brandy, port, and liqueurs. We started with champagne for the Christmas toast. Although I drank very little alcohol I was persuaded to take a sip.

Tom's relatives looked at me with curiosity. 'You are the Indian friend we have been hearing so much about.' I smiled but felt like an exhibit. Tom had explained to me that he had invited his five cousins because they lived on their own.

Tom's mother had spent the whole of Christmas Eve preparing the meal. I knew the menu but was shocked by the sight. I was not expecting to see a huge roasted bird filled with stuffing. Tom was the carver. When he sharpened the knife, started cutting large slices of turkey, and scooped out the stuffing with a spoon, I wanted to get up and run away. In India we never serve whole animals or birds; they are cut into small pieces and hidden by the curry sauce. But I forced myself to stay at the table and gradually settled down to enjoy the food. Roast potatoes and sprouts were served with the turkey, care being taken to give everyone equal portions of white and dark meat.

The Christmas pudding arrived. The lights were put out and the curtains drawn. Tom poured brandy over the pudding and lit it. Everyone applauded as blue flames flickered. What a waste of good brandy, I thought. It was used as medicine in my village.

We slowly ate our way through the vast quantities of food as though we had never eaten before, pausing briefly to hear the Queen's speech. Tom's mother produced a box of crackers. We pulled them, put on the paper hats, and read out the mottoes. Then the ceremony of the presents began. Everybody behaved like little children, opening parcels and reading the messages. Tom read out a letter from his aunt in Australia sending greetings to the family.

I was touched by the present from Tom's mother. It was a pullover and a pair of gloves she had knitted herself. I had seen her knitting but had not realized she was doing it for me. 'It's not the present but the thought that counts,' Tom's mother said.

In the early evening we went out for a walk. The streets were deserted, the houses had their curtains drawn but I could see lights filtering through. In some windows decorated Christmas trees were clearly visible. For one day the family had come together and the outside world was forgotten. When we returned to the flat we found tea and Christmas cake on the table, prepared by Tom's mother. I had presented her with a tin of Indian tea, which she served with great pride. But I heard some of the relatives complaining it was not strong enough for them. I knew tea drinking was a ritual in England but very few seemed to bother about the quality. Their taste was affected by drinking too much 'English tea' and they were unable to appreciate the taste of pure Indian tea.

When the relatives left in the evening I heard one say to Tom's mother, 'Hope to see you next Christmas, if not before.'

Do they only meet at Christmas, I wondered.

I had wanted to make a film to show people the beauty and simplicity of life in my village. By chance, in the summer of 1980, I met a BBC producer in the house of a friend. A few days later he telephoned to say that he had enjoyed reading my book, *My Village, My Life*, and thought it would make an excellent film for television. We met a number of times to discuss the project.

During my annual visit to the village in the spring of 1981, the producer came there to do research and make preliminary arrangements for the film. I spent several days looking after him, introducing him to the villagers and government officials in Delhi and Orissa.

Foreign film-makers are required to sign an undertaking to observe certain regulations laid down by the Government of India. First, the script must be approved by the Government of India. Second, a liaison officer, appointed by the Government of India, must be present during the entire duration of filming in India and the team must agree 'to abide by his advice regarding the filming of any particular scene'. The team must also 'meet the expenses for the travel and stay of the liaison officer'. 'Failure to abide by the liaison officer's advice regarding shooting of any particular scene may result in the immediate stoppage of any further filming and confiscation of the exposed film.' Third, a final rough cut of the film must be shown 'to a representative of the Government of India at least two weeks before final telecasting screening, also furnishing in advance a full translation in England of the commentary, and further agreement to abide by such advice as may be given by the representative with regard to alteration in or excision of such parts of the film and the commentary as may affect a balanced and accurate presentation of the theme of the film'.

The producer's script was not accepted by the government of India because it did not give a balanced view. He came to me for help and showed me a letter which he had received from Delhi: 'In our opinion the portrayal of the village in your script is rather static and it does not show in any way how more than thirty years of development planning initiated by the Government has transformed the village. To that extent the portrait lacks balance and we would like you to restore this balance after due consultations with Mr Mohanti.'

The producer said that the BBC had invited me to make this film about my village through my eyes, based on my book. The BBC would provide me with all the facilities and help me to realize my vision of the village. The film would be the BBC's contribution to the Festival of India, and apart from being shown on television, it would also be shown at the National Film Theatre. He also said he did not want a liaison officer and asked me to write a letter to the Government of India.

I hoped the film would help the villagers and by showing it I would be able to collect money for my village development project. So I wrote a letter to the Government of India. In it I said: '[The producer] wants the film to be about myself and my village, seen through my eyes. It will show what the village means to me and to the other villagers; the family life and human relationships, the sense of belonging to a community, the dignity of the individual, the arts and crafts, and above all the beauty of village life. The development since 1947 will be unavoidable – electricity, improved farming methods, and the express highway which has connected the village with the outside world. By describing my childhood and showing the village as it is today, the film will reveal the developments which have taken place since Independence. For example, I received a loan scholarship from the Orissa Government to study architecture in Bombay in 1955. This changed my life and would have been unthinkable during the British Raj. Cholera and smallpox are under control and modern drugs have reduced suffering and raised the expectancy of life. But I have to be careful not to appear to make government propaganda or give too romantic a view of my village. That would lower the quality and importance of the film.

'[The producer] is one of the most sensitive film-makers I have met here. I can communicate with him. He came to my village last March and spent one week there. He liked the village and the villagers liked him and accepted him as a friend. He believes that the village helped him to understand the importance of basic things in life and that it has a lot to offer the West. I would like to assure you that the film will give a positive and perceptive picture of Indian village life although the film is only about one particular village.

'I understand that it is usual for a liaison officer from the Ministry of External Affairs to be attached to a foreign film unit. As I will be present throughout the making of this film in India I wonder if a liaison officer is really necessary. The presence of a government official could easily inhibit the villagers and make them self-conscious. As you know, I love my village and would not allow anything to be done which would offend the villagers.'

I received a prompt reply from the Government of India saying they would do their best to reconcile my sensitivities with their procedural requirements.

On the strength of my letter all the necessary permissions were given without the usual bureaucratic delay and my request not to have a liaison officer was granted. My friends in the government departments went out of their way to help my making arrangements for accommodation and transport of the BBC team.

No money was discussed, although I had worked on the project for over one year without a formal contract. I had not asked for payment, nor had the BBC offered me any. But I believed the BBC paid its contributors in a fair way. I was brought up in a tradition where, if you invited somebody, you looked after him in every way.

After I had made all the arrangements for the film, which spread over nearly fifteen months, I suddenly received a telephone call from a woman in the BBC Contracts Division.

'I understand you want to make a film and you don't have an agent.'

'Yes.'

'We will offer you a fee of £1,600.' She outlined the work I would have to do.

I said I would think about it and let her know. After discussions with friends who had worked in television, I thought £2,000 and the rights to show the film in cinemas would be adequate.

When I phoned her she said she would have to talk to the producer.

'Why? Has he suggested an amount?' I asked.

She giggled.

'I have been meeting him frequently. Why didn't he tell me about it himself?'

'That's how it is done inside the BBC,' she said.

I considered the producer as a friend. 'If he thinks it is the right amount, that's all right by me,' I said.

The next day the producer took me to lunch at a fashionable restaurant. When I told him what the Contracts Division had said he denied having suggested an amount.

A friend introduced me to an agent who said it was not a fair contract. But the BBC argued that I had already accepted its offer on the phone and threatened to withdraw the project. I found it most embarrassing as the film was planned to be shown during the Festival of India and all the arrangements had been made. I volunteered to give my services free if it would help my village.

The executive producer came to see me. He was an extremely sensitive person and had made a film in India before. He persuaded me to accept the offer with certain amendments to the contract. He also promised to give me any help I needed in the making of the film. I was assured that the villagers would be paid for their contribution.

I had an exhibition of my paintings in Tokyo. On the way I stopped in Delhi for ten days, getting all the government clearances for the film and making final arrangements for the travel and accommodation of the crew, so that when they arrived they would not face any problems.

Unfortunately, a week after my arrival in Tokyo I was taken ill, an after-effect of my attack in Wapping. I was advised complete rest by the doctors but I wanted to make the film and kept my original arrangements with the BBC.

When we arrived in the village with all the government clearances and no liaison officer, the producer handed me a script and a schedule and demanded that I organize the villagers to act accordingly. The film was going to be a portrait of my village through his eyes, not mine. The BBC was doing me, my village, and India a favour by making this film, I was told. He wanted the film to show me arriving in the village by bus, being greeted by the villagers, taking off my Western clothes, putting on Indian dress, and then going round introducing the village and the villagers – in other words, a typical BBC documentary. I wanted the film to be an honest and authentic portrait of the village without me standing between it and the viewers, giving them an opportunity to get into its heart.

I saw the film as a work of art, depicting aspects of the village which have influenced me as an artist and writer, showing both its beauty and its problems.

I ignored the producer's orders and tried to direct the film, but he started threatening me, saying he would return to England with the crew.

I was feeling extremely tired after my illness in Japan and had the sole responsibility of organizing the villagers for filming. They do not allow non-Hindus near the sacred places and into their homes. But the BBC team was accepted by the villagers because they thought they were my friends.

After a young woman was filmed, her husband was bitten by a snake. Luckily the snake was not poisonous but the villagers thought the BBC had brought bad luck. I spent long hours persuading them and got their full co-operation. But I found it difficult to get the help and understanding of the producer. When it came to paying the villagers he started bargaining, even refusing to pay ten rupees to the taxi driver for his meal. A seventy-year-old Brahmin, who spent three days in the river being filmed, was offered £6 for his remuneration. Yet the producer and crew drank fifty bottles of beer a night, costing at least £50, and a man was employed at £20 a day to ferry the beer by taxi from a town sixty miles away.

I tried to explain the village customs to the producer and how you can offend people by offering them less than they deserve. 'I haven't got the time to understand your village,' he said. The next day the taxi driver delivered a letter to me at my house. It was from the producer withdrawing the project.

I had promised the executive producer that I would complete the film and did so with the help of the crew. The villagers decided not to accept any money from the producer and authorized me to act on their behalf. When the team left after two weeks the villagers gave them a farewell reception and the children produced a play.

I got the film cleared through the government officials in Orissa and the BBC crew returned to England. Then I received a letter from a friend in London saying that the

BBC had the right to show the film the way it wanted to without consulting me. There were twelve hours of filming and I was concerned that if any aspect of life in my village was shown out of context it would give a distorted image. So I wrote a letter to the Government of India who made it a condition that I should be present at the preview to the Indian High Commission.

In London I met the executive producer to discuss the shape of the film. He said he had known the producer for twenty-five years and had a sense of loyalty towards him. But he agreed to listen to both our views and then decide.

Surprisingly, the executive producer agreed to all my suggestions as against those of the producer, who gradually withdrew. I spent two months editing the film, giving it a shape, selecting the music, and writing and narrating the commentary. The executive producer was like a teacher, helping me patiently at every stage. When I discussed the payment of the villagers with him I received a letter from the BBC saying that all financial matters should be settled between my agent and the Contracts Division.

A press preview was promised but it was withdrawn. The absence of a producer and editor on the credit titles would give bad publicity to the BBC, I was told. On my insistence a preview was arranged only a day before the broadcast. Nobody noticed the omissions. The film was shown on BBC 2 on 25 March 1982 during the first week of the Festival of India, and was highly praised by the critics and the viewers.

Soon afterwards I received a letter from my agent telling me that the BBC Contracts Division did not want to get involved with the fees to the villagers and the Head of the Arts Department was looking after it. When I took the matter up with him I received a letter saying that the BBC's representative in Delhi had verified that the villagers had already been paid. I knew it was not true and wrote a letter to the Chairman of the BBC on 23 July. Instead of receiving a reply from him I got a letter from the BBC solicitor.

A few days later I received a letter from a friend in the village. It said that on 27 July a BBC official arrived in the village with an interpreter and another Indian, who was presented to the villagers as the District Collector. They told the villagers that I had sent money for them and distributed 950 rupees (£55) among a few contributors who were present and took their receipts. When I wrote back saying the money had not come from me the villagers returned it to the BBC and asked for their receipts. When my agent discussed payment for my extra work the BBC pointed out that my contract read, 'For all work necessary to complete a fifty minute film', and when I wanted to show the film to the villagers the BBC said I would have to buy a copy and quoted £1,250 plus VAT for a 16-mm film and £380 plus VAT for a video cassette.

Two months later I was intrigued to read an article in *The Times* headed, 'Brideshead repainted, thanks to Granada.' It said, 'Castle Howard, the architect Vanbrugh's first masterpiece, was used as Brideshead in Granada television's dramatization of Evelyn Waugh's novel. The fee which George Howard, chairman of the BBC, squeezed out of his commercial rivals for lending his house has provided the finance to realize a dream of creating new rooms.'

But my dream of helping the village through the film did not come true. I sat in my studio reflecting on the film. For the BBC it was only one of many films it makes every year. For me it was the most important. I had kept all my promises to the BBC in spite of immense difficulties. I was brought up in a culture where the spoken word is as important as the written word. I felt all the problems I had faced were worthwhile when people came up to me in the street and said how much they had enjoyed my film. Several teachers wrote to me saying that they wanted to show the film to their students to help them understand India. Tears came to my eyes when I read what the *Daily Telegraph* critic had written: 'Never before, in my fallible memory of television past, has the audience been able to see a remote primitive Indian village through the eyes of one of its sons; one who regards it, even when he is in England, especially when he is in England, as the home he can never leave.'

I watched the tree in the yard change through the seasons. In the winter, without leaves, it looked sad, but with the coming of spring, buds gradually opened out like flowers and turned into leaves. In the summer the tree was full again and, as autumn approached, the leaves turned yellow and brown and started to fall. It was a resting place for all kinds of birds who filled the air with their songs. Pigeons danced on the slate roof and when it rained and water cascaded, they took shelter on the drainpipe outside my neighbour's house. The back wall in summer was covered by a creeper which turned into deep red in the autumn. But the first wind of the winter proved too strong for the delicate leaves. Suddenly the wall was bare again. It was time for me to leave for India.

Extracts from *Through Brown Eyes* (Oxford University Press).

The Indian Novel:
a New Literary Genre?

GANESWAR MISHRA

The two dominant forms of narrative in India, until the novel and the short story were borrowed by Indians from the West more than a century ago, were the folktale and the *purana*. Both the forms are a part of oral tradition. In the West the oral tradition of storytelling is virtually extinct now. But in India, where most of the people are illiterate, and sophisticated mass media have made little impact on rural communities, the oral forms of narrative remain extremely important even today.

An Indian folktale, generally, is either a debased or derived version of some Sanskrit parable or fable of the medieval period, such as *Panchatantra*, *Hitopadesha* or *Kathasaritsagara* or the invention of some anonymous local genius. It is a prose narrative but often particular proverbs, riddles and verses go with a particular folktale and serve as an aid to memory. The *purana* is essentially a religious work based on the *Ramayana* or the *Mahabharata*; the folktale is not, though both are didactic and allegorical in nature. Whereas the folktale is narrated from memory usually by grand-parents or elderly persons to the children, the *purana* is read out by the brahmin, from a printed book or from palm-leaf manuscripts and interpreted to an adult audience. The *purana* is a verse narrative, but the interpretation which forms a part of the ritualistic reading of the *purana* is in prose. There is, however, considerable overlapping between the two forms. One can always find within the *purana* a number of folktales prevalent in the language area in which it is composed. On the other hand, many folktales may be based on puranic themes.

After the age of Sanskrit epics and with the emergence of the Prakrit languages, the folktale and the *purana* came to dominate the Indian cultural scene for a thousand years or so until Indians were exposed to English language and literature in the nineteenth century. A series of epoch-making events took place in India between 1830 and 1880: the starting of the printing machine; the compilation on modern lines of grammars and dictionaries in Indian languages; the collection of folktales; the imparting of Western science and culture in the English language; the establishment of colleges and universities and so on. This was also the period when the first Indian novel, the first Indian poem in blank-verse – almost all the modern forms of Indian literature – were composed. The novel, and all forms of prose literature in the modern sense, were imitated by Indians often with considerable success. But the abrupt transition from the traditional forms of literature to the modern ones has not always been smooth or convincing.

As happens in any period of transition, the Indian authors in the nineteenth century were not very sure of the nature of this transition and its subsequent effect on the form and content of their writing. Few seemed to realise that the Western form which had already had a century-old history and had evolved in a totally different social and cultural milieu, was not a very adequate form to articulate the prevailing Indian ethos.

When Bankim Chandra Chatterjee, the most important Indian novelist of the nineteenth century, started writing, he broke away from the traditional narrative forms in two significant ways: first, he wrote all his works in prose; secondly, he expressed a deep social concern. He was a conscious artist and realised that the conventional themes and forms had already outlived their utility and that the possibilities of the new forms such as the novel should be explored.[1] But in spite of his reaction against traditional themes and techniques in literature, Chatterjee himself, at his best, was somewhere between the modern and the conventional and his work is a curious blending of the Indian folk narrative and the Western novel.

Rajmohan's Wife (1864) is Bankim Chandra Chatterjee's first novel and the only one written in English. Though not particularly remarkable as a work of art, it can safely be taken as a representative novel of the nineteenth century in respect of form and language, characterisation and point of view.

Rajmohan's Wife deals with the suffering of a Hindu housewife, a recurring theme in Indian fiction in the nineteenth and the early twentieth century. Chatterjee is a very contemporary author, deeply involved in the social problems of his time and one of his favourite themes is the emancipation of Hindu housewives from their age-old suffering and superstition. He is realistic enough, in his novel, to focus upon the gloomy and morbid aspect of the *zenana* (the women's quarters) and does not romanticise or idealise the traditional life of the Hindu housewife in the manner of the narrator of the folktale or the *purana*. His picture of the *zenana* as described in the chapter, 'A Letter – A Visit to the *Zenana*', is no less accurate and realistic than, say, a similar description in a twentieth century novel:

> ... Madhav therefore immediately hurried into the inner apartments where he found it no very easy task to make himself heard in that busy hour of zenana life. There was a servant woman, black, rotund and eloquent, demanding the transmission to her hands of sundry articles of domestic use, without however

making it at all intelligible to whom her demands were particularly addressed. There was another, who boasted similar blessed corporal dimensions, but who had thought it beneath her dignity to shelter them from view; and was busily employed, broomstick in hand, in demolishing the little mountains of the skins and stems of sundry culinary vegetables which decorated the floors, and against which the half-naked dame never aimed a blow but coupled it with a curse on those whose duty it had been to prepare the said vegetables for dressing.

A third had ensconced herself in that corner of the yard which formed the grand receptacle of household filth, and was employing all her energies in scouring some brass pots;...[2]

However, one does not come across many passages in the novel, like the one quoted above, suggesting Chatterjee's attempt to portray a realistic picture of society. The plot is very well contrived, and the message is made obvious by the authorial comments from time to time and the 'Conclusion' at the end of the novel. One character is clearly contrasted with another; thus if one is a noble man, the other is a rogue and so forth. The situations in which characters find themselves seem predestined and conventional (a beautiful and virtuous woman married to a very cruel husband, for instance). Whenever there is a crisis, it is resolved by some supernatural agent or as a matter of chance. Many of the images are hackneyed and muchused in Indian folktales and *puranas*. Throughout the novel the author is conscious that he is telling a story to his readers and the novelist-reader relation from time to time reminds one of the narrator/reciter-audience situation in an Indian village when a folktale is narrated or a *purana* is read out. All these characteristics of the novel suggest its closeness to the folk form of narrative.

Rajmohan's wife, Matangini, is the central character in the novel. The novelist, after describing the small village on the bank of the river Madhumati, the locale of the story – a conventional way of beginning a folk or puranic tale – proceeds to introduce the heroine and her companion at length. 'Let us describe them both at this place,'[3] he tells us as a folktale narrator or a *puranakara* would have done before describing a goddess or a mythical beauty. He also follows the folk convention by describing Kanak, Matangini's maid servant, as less beautiful than Matangini herself.

'The rays of the setting sun had vanished from the tops of the coconut palms. But night had not yet descended on the earth. It was at this time that Kanak and her companion were returning home.'[4] This is how the second chapter opens; again, a conventional way of starting a tale or an episode, by referring to nature. Five of the twenty-one chapters in the novel begin with an elaborate description of the natural surroundings, and human action described against such surroundings seems to be in perfect harmony with it. The assumption of such harmony is a convention in folk literature and is based on the Hindu idea of viewing human action as a part of the cosmic design of things.

Matangini's suffering at the hands of Rajmohan, her cruel husband, is the central theme of the story. Matangini's suffering and Rajmohan's cruelty are described unequivocally and the characters, in their extreme virtue and cruelty, tend to be more symbolic than real. The plot is ingeniously contrived and the characters are made to fit the plot. None of the characters seems to grow in the course of the events though many significant events follow one after another in the novel. The novelist's tone of resignation often suggests that the characters could not be otherwise, a suggestion very compatible with the Hindu idea of *karma* or rebirth. In *puranas* and folktales, man is hardly viewed as a free or liberated being, the possibility of his individual growth thus being almost denied. The interplay of character and situation to make a character grow assumes that the individual is to a large extent a product of his environment. In folktales and *puranas* characters are 'born' and not 'made' by circumstances and are often categorised as Gods (*Suras*) and Demons (*Asuras*). Chatterjee, though concerned with a contemporary issue, does not portray Matangini as a living woman, with her human flaws, but as a *Devi* or Goddess. All the rest of the characters are similarly portrayed in broad outlines, either as good or bad; and the conflict between characters seems to be the conventional conflict between two clearly defined opposite forces.

It seems logical in the context of the Hindu idea of predestination that the virtuous should be protected and the wicked punished in this world. And Chatterjee follows this logic which brings his work closer to the *purana* and the folktale than to the Western novel. To get his point through, Chatterjee takes recourse to the conventional device of introducing miracles and chance elements which at once makes the story improbable and even fantastic. Destiny is an important character in *Rajmohan's Wife* playing a determining role through various agents, though Chatterjee does not attribute a human form to this character as the folk narrators sometimes do in the form of Niyati or some supernatural being.

The didactic note is palpably obvious throughout the novel, and through his comments and addresses to the 'dear reader':

> The reader need not be informed that with much of the subject of this interesting dialogue, he is already acquainted.[5]

> The scoundrel was preaching philosophy to the great man! And, dear reader, was he very wrong?[6]

Such novelist-reader dialogues make the reader feel the presence of the novelist, and this situation is not very different from that of the folk narrator sitting beside his or her listeners and narrating the story.

Between Chatterjee's *Rajmohan's Wife* and the twentieth-century novels of Raja Rao, R.K. Narayan, Bhabani Bhattacharya and Sudhin Ghose there is a gap of half a century and the novelists have shown, like their counterparts anywhere in the world, an increasingly greater bias towards realism. This awareness, however, has not resulted in any substantial change in the novel form in India; that is, novelists like Chatterjee and Narayan, in spite of their concern for different sets of issues, have remained surprisingly close to each other in the treatment of their form. The form of the novel has not changed as much as its theme, and this fact clearly shows the impact of the traditional folk narrative forms on the novel. And the impact of which Chatterjee was hardly aware has not only been obvious to modern novelists, but almost all of them have emphasised, in their own ways, the appropriateness of the folk forms in the modern context, and have suggested perhaps the blending of the folk form and the Western novel. Raja Rao's *Kanthapura* (1938), the most deliberate and the most important attempt made so far in Indian English fiction to incorporate a folk form in the body of the novel, has this in the 'Author's Foreword':

> There is no village in India, however mean, that has not a rich *sthala-purana*, or legendary history, of its own. Some god or godlike hero has passed by the village – Rama might have rested under this pipal-tree, Sita might have dried her clothes, after her bath, on this yellow stone, or the Mahatma himself, on one of his many pilgrimages through the country, might have slept in this hut, the low one, by the village gate. In this way the past mingles with the present, and the gods mingle with men to make the repertory of your grandmother always bright...

> It may have been told of an evening, when as the dusk falls, and through the sudden quiet, lights leap up in house after house, and stretching her bedding on the veranda, a grandmother might have told you, newcomer, the sad tale of her village.[7]

Kanthapura is the sad story of an Indian village that was completely destroyed by the British police for participating in the Indian freedom movement. A grandmother of Kanthapura who survives and takes shelter in a neighbouring village, narrates her experience before a number of women.

This is an excellent example of a contemporary reality being cast in the folk narrative form, and this is how an average Indian would perhaps narrate his or her experience. This narrative can well be an episode in the line of episodes in the Indian folk and puranic tradition. The contemporary ceases to be contemporary in the way it is treated and turns into the universal.

The village-grandmother narrator does not discriminate between the past and the present, between myth and reality. The struggle for independence, for her, is no different from the struggle between the Gods and the Demons, just as the birth of the Mahatma is hardly different from the birth of Rama or Krishna as described in the *puranas*:

> And lo! when the Sage was still partaking of the pleasures Brahma offered him in hospitality, there was born in a family in Gujerat a son such as the world has never beheld. As soon as he came forth, the four wide walls began to shine like the Kingdom of the Sun, and hardly was he in the cradle than he began to lisp the language of wisdom. You remember how Krishna, when he was but a babe of four, had begun to fight against demons and had killed the serpent Kali. So too our Mohandas began to fight against the enemies of the country. And as he grew up, and after he was duly shaven for the hair ceremony, he began to go out into the villages and assemble people and talk to them, and his voice was so pure, his forehead so brilliant with wisdom, that men followed him, more and more men followed him as they did Krishna the flute-player; and so he goes from village to village to slay the serpent of the foreign rule.[8]

In his introduction to *Gods, Demons and Others*, R.K. Narayan makes the following observations regarding the traditional Indian narrative:

> Every story has implicit in it a philosophical or moral significance, and an underlining of the distinction between good and evil. To the storyteller and his audience the tales are so many chronicles of personalities who inhabited this world at some remote time, and whose lives are worth understanding, and hence

form part of human history rather than fiction. In every story, since goodness triumphs in the end, there is no tragedy in the Greek sense; the curtain never comes down *finally* on corpses strewn about the stage. The sufferings of the meek and the saintly are temporary, even as the triumph of the demon is; everyone knows this. Everything is bound to come out right in the end; if not immediately, at least in a thousand or ten thousand years; if not in this world, at least in other worlds.[9]

These words can serve in some way as an introduction to Narayan's own world of fiction as well. Narayan's moral vision and expression of concern for the contemporary in relation to the eternal are clearly puranic. In each of his novels, the story ends either with the elimination of the character representing evil or the elimination of the evil in the character.

Narayan's *The Man-eater of Malgudi* is an example of a puranic rendering of a story of modern India. It deals with the conflict between Vasu, the champion of all Western values as he understands them and the Malgudi society representing traditional India. Vasu is highly educated and full of ideas for the industrialisation and technological progress of the country. But in his utter disregard for the human beings around him and in his lust and greed, he clearly resembles the puranic demon or *rakshasa*. And this is what Sastri, the pious brahmin in the novel, has to say about the fate of the *rakshasa*: 'Every rakshasa gets swollen with his ego. He thinks he is invincible, beyond every law. But sooner or later something or other will destroy him.'[10]

When at the zenith of power and prosperity, Vasu, like the *rakshasa* Bhasmasura, suddenly kills himself and the evil is eliminated, miraculously, from Malgudi society.

The structure of the novel, *The Man-eater of Malgudi*, is puranic too. Two important motifs are suggested in the opening of the *purana*: firstly, the world seems peaceful and tranquil to the sages until the visitor arrives and disturbs that peace by narrating stories of demons and so forth; secondly, the narrative invariably assumes the form of a dialogue. Vasu, coming from a distant place, disturbs the peace of Malgudi and the story is narrated by Nataraj, who himself is an important character in the novel. In the *purana* and the folktale, the narrator is often a participant in the story and both in *Kanthapura* and in *The Man-eater of Malgudi* the novelists follow this convention.

In the West, the rise of the novel had a lot to do with the acceptance of individualism and privacy as important values. But in India where the individual is supposed to live for the group – joint family, caste or whatever – such values are alien to the masses. An art-form is intimately linked with the ethos of the society from within which it grows and in Indian society, therefore, communal art forms such as the reading of the *purana* or the narrating of the folktale seem to be natural and genuine. The printed word does not mean a thing to the majority of Indians anyway. And a novelist writing about the ordinary Indian cannot ignore the art-forms in which the ordinary Indian feels at home.

After independence, interestingly, there has been a rapid expansion of English language and literature as well as of Western values in India, on the one hand, and an increasingly greater emphasis on folk forms of art and literature, on the other. One can reasonably hope, therefore, that the Indian novel is going to be a blend of the Western novel and the Indian traditional narrative, giving rise to a new literary genre.

NOTES

1. See Bankim Chandra Chatterjee's 'A Popular Literature for Bengali' and 'Bengali Literature', in J.C. Bagal, ed., *Bankim Rachanavali* (Calcutta: Sahitya Sansad, 1969).
2. Ibid., pp. 17-18.
3. Ibid., p. 2.
4. Ibid., p. 5.

5. Ibid., p. 48.
6. Ibid., p. 86.
7. *Kanthapura* (New York: New Directions, 1967), pp. vii-viii.
8. Ibid., pp. 11-12.
9. *Gods, Demons and Others* (New York: The Viking Press, 1969), pp. 4-5.
0. *The Man-eater of Malgudi* (Mysore: Indian Thought Publications, 1973), p. 96.

Mulk Raj Anand:
Stages in a Confession

ALASTAIR NIVEN

It is a little impertinent of me to be speaking about one of
India's major writers, Mulk Raj Anand, in the presence of
another distinguished Indian artist and writer, Prafulla
Mohanti, and of the critic Ganeswar Mishra, both of whom
have as high an opinion of Anand's work as I do. In this
they are perhaps unusual. It is not uncommon to meet
Indian intellectuals who regard Anand at quite a low level
at the moment. Meanwhile, his reputation outside India
has faded. Yet during the 1930's and 1940's, anyone in the
literary world, particularly in left-wing intellectual circles
in Europe, would have been aware of Mulk Raj Anand. He
was so closely associated with the leading writers of that
distant time, that it is sometimes hard to believe that he is
not only still alive, but creatively active. He was born in
central Punjab in 1905 and to some extent his position in
Indian letters is analogous with that of George Bernard
Shaw at the end of his long life.

Anand played as prominent a role in Indian society,
nationalism and development as Shaw did in British society in the twentieth century and he is as prolific a writer.
Although he has never been a playwright, he is the author
of fifteen full-length novels, and many shorter ones, several

groups of short stories, innumerable essays, starting off with the famous essay on Persian painting (for an exhibition of Persian painting at Burlington House, London, in 1930) and he continues to this day to write provocative essays with titles like 'Is There Such a Thing as Indian Civilisation?'. He has access to the highest reaches of the Congress parties and Indian society, and one of his great boasts is of his rather ambivalent relationship with Indira Gandhi, who called him 'Uncle Mulk'. He is a prolific correspondent: anyone who has had any dealings with him in a critical capacity receives bundles of letters by return! I doubt if I shall make my fortune out of Mulk Raj Anand's letters, because I suspect it is quite rare in India not to have received one, just as they used to say in England that it was much rarer to have an unsigned edition of an Edward Heath book than a signed one!

Mulk Raj Anand was brought up in Amritsar, the Sikh centre which has been so sadly in the news in recent years because of the horrifying events which have taken place around the Golden Temple. Anand is not a Sikh, although he did have Sikh relations, and he was brought up in a fairly humble household, his father being a sepoy. He was related to a traditional coppersmith family and grew up speaking Punjabi. He learned English at school at quite a young age and it was mainly through the medium of English that he established himself as a writer, although he has sometimes written in Punjabi or translated into it. His use of English is greatly affected by Punjabi rhythms and metaphors, especially in his rendering of dialogue.

He first came to the notice of people in the literary field in 1935, with the publication of *Untouchable*, still his best-known novel.[1] A short book, it describes the events in a single day of a latrine cleaner, someone who has the lowest function in Indian society, below caste. In describing in fictional form the events of one day in the life of Bakha, the untouchable latrine-cleaner, Anand managed to reach the heart of the tragedy of the dispossessed in Indian society. He had great difficulty in getting the novel published. Who would take seriously in 1935 an Indian writer using the English language, not altogether elegantly, to describe the fortunes of someone whose work was to clear up the shit? The book was rejected by nineteen publishers, and only finally published because E.M. Forster managed to prevail upon Lawrence and Wishart to produce it, providing he himself wrote an introduction to it. This procedure has been the story of many Indian writers, certainly in Anand's generation, who have only managed to achieve recognition because of the patronage of major European writers. R.K. Narayan benefited from the patronage of Graham Greene and G.V. Desani from Anthony Burgess. Each of these writers wrote about the daily experiences of India, far from the affairs of the Mogul empire or from metaphysics and mysticism. There was no exoticism in their work and none of that mellow nostalgia for the past which had been the condition of so many European works about India. In his preface to *Two Leaves in a Bud*, a later novel which deals with the iniquities of how the tea plantations are organised, Anand defined what he was trying to do in his writing:

> Until I began to write about the outcasts, the pariahs, the peasants and bottom dogs of my country, and to resurrect them from the obscure lanes and alleys of the hamlets, villages and small towns, nothing very much had been heard or written about them in polite literature, in the languages of our sub-continent or in English. The novels of Bankhim Chander were mainly romantic historical narratives, à la Scott. In the work of Sarat Chanda Chatterjee the lower middle class, constituted by clerks, small merchants and humble folk, began to appear as human beings. And J. Premchand, author of *The Gift of a Cow*, wrote about the defeated peasantry and small peoples of Uttar Pradesh with a poignant tenderness. I found myself going beyond the work of those three writers, because the world I knew best was the microcosm of the outcasts and peasants and soldiers and working people. Of course, I am of my time and the atmosphere of the thirties, with it's hangover from crises, influenced me strongly. But contrary to superficial allegations, there was not much self-

conscious proletarianism in my attitude, as there was in many of the middle-class writers of western Europe, simply for the reason that I *was* the son of a coppersmith-turned-soldier and of a peasant mother and could have written only of their lives, because I knew them intimately. In so far, however, as my work broke new ground, and represented a departure from the works of previous Indian fiction, where the pariahs and bottom dogs had not been allowed to enter the sacred precincts of the novel, or their reality, it seemed to become significant and to draw the attention of the critics, particularly in Europe, which only knew Omar Khayam, Li Po and Tagore but very little or nothing about the sordid and colourful lives of the millions of Asia.[2]

Anand has continued to write about 'the sordid and colourful lives of the millions' ever since. Because he advocated Socialist prescriptions in some of his work of the 1940's he has sometimes been dismissed for purely political considerations. It is worth, even in this doctrinaire phase of his career, exploring beneath the polemic. There is a disarming awareness in Anand, however, that by choosing to write in English he runs the risk of marginalising himself from the main traditions of Indian literature. He says,

And though our writing in English, together with the work of Anglo-Indian or Eurasian writers, is strictly not a stream of Indian writing, but a kind of regional branch of English literature, it is yet, if we are not too journalistic in our approach, a part of the Indian cultural development and it has its value, if only as an interpretive literature of the most vital character.[3]

Perhaps, however, it is irrelevant to worry too much about his centrality within Indian literature. He would like to be regarded as a world writer and at his peak that is how he was received, being translated into over fourteen languages, being honoured in many countries of the world, being nominated, though not yet receiving, the Nobel Prize, and being regarded until about 1953 as a very considerable international figure. Since 1953, when he published *Private Life of an Indian Prince,*[4] which many Anand critics regard as his masterpiece, but which is unusual among his works in that it deals with the aristocracy and its decline in India rather than with the peasant class, Anand has had no *new* novel published outside India, but has continued to write prolifically within India. Much of this work has been a sequence of confessional novels.

The first of these appeared in 1951 and was called *Seven Summers*, an account of childhood up to the age of seven.[5] Followed in 1968 by a very long novel called *Morning Face*[6] (we pick up the reference to the 'seven ages of man' speech in *As You Like It*), they begin a planned sequence of seven novels, covering seven phases of his own life in a thinly disguised autobiographical form. In 1976 came *Confession of a Lover*[7] and then *The Bubble*, 1984.[8] This last novel was launched in the presence of the Vice-President of India which is interesting simply because it suggests that the rehabilitation of Anand as a major writer may be under way in India. Certainly British publishers have suddenly started to take an interest in him again. Penguin and The Bodley Head have brought out re-prints of his work and there are discussions with Heinemann to produce the autobiographical novels. When I was writing a short book on Anand I regarded these autobiographical confessional novels as the key to his work.[9] Without intending to flatter him, I felt that access to Anand's *oeuvre* was through what he had to say about his own life. He himself certainly believed that to be so because, when my book came out he wrote to me and said that at last someone was approaching his work the right way round, looking at it through him, the man, and not through what he had to say of a political or didactic nature. But these autobiographical novels are not well known in India, perhaps because they are immensely long (*Morning Face* runs to over 600 pages, *Confession of a Lover* is very long too, *The Bubble* is 603 pages) and they have not yet been published in Europe.

They take very different forms. *Seven Summers* is written in the rather simple reminiscing style of an adult consciously looking back on childhood, but with something of that kind of conscious naiveté of vision that Michael Anthony achieves in *The Year in San Fernando* or Edwin Muir in the opening chapter of his autobiography in which he was describing his upbringing in Orkney. As the novels proceed they introduce more and more documentation of a kind that was actually being created in the period about which the novel is taking place. Let me try and be more explicit about that. There is an element, to use a fashionable word which is increasingly used of television series, of 'faction' about these recent novels, particularly in *Confession of a Lover* and *The Bubble*. Woven into them are diary entries, correspondence and conversations written down on the day they take place which come directly to us now from the moment that they were happening. We have, in *The Bubble*, letters to friends back in India, scribbles put down on paper of conversations that Anand wrote as he left the room, having met Bertrand Russell or Forster or Virginia Woolf, and these now, sixty years later, reappear in the novel. It makes an astonishingly vivid but obviously to some extent unedited account of what it was like to be a young Indian both in India and in London at this period. I am talking of 1921, when *Confession of a Lover* opens, through to 1930 when *The Bubble* ends. As an adjunct to these books, particularly to *The Bubble*, Anand has produced a rather slight collection of conversations in Bloomsbury, a recollection of conversations that he had with such people as Bonamy Dobrée, T.S. Eliot, Herbert Read, Aldous Huxley and Middleton Murray, the literati of the Bloomsbury circle.[10] The link character of this sequence of autobiographical novels is obviously Anand himself. I am not one of those people who wants to identify the *Bildungsroman* form too literally with the author of the work. For example, I would regard it as mistaken to read *Sons and Lovers* as Lawrence's autobiography. It has elements of Lawrence, but it is profoundly a work of the creative imagination. I would be much less insistent in saying that of the autobiographical sequence by Anand. Krishan Chanda Azad, the main character, is clearly Mulk Raj Anand himself. The family relationships, the circumstances of Krishan's career, his friendships, both with ordinary people and with prominent people in Indian and British society, are those of Anand himself.

The novels only leave northern India in *The Bubble*, so the first three take place in the area of the Punjab centring on Amritsar and Peshawar. The first two books, though separated from each other in their dates of publication by seventeen years, form a continuous narrative. They could be read straight through as though they were one novel. If there is an obvious unifying metaphysic in these two novels, it is encapsulated in the brief snatch of a Rilke poem with which Anand heads one section of *Morning Face*: 'Loneliness, vast inner loneliness,/ Is the lot of Mankind.' We also trace in *Seven Summers* and *Morning Face* the birth of Anand's socialist humanism. In the person of Krishan, we see him early on sharing his father's cynical attitude towards religion. But he never ceases at the same time to venerate his deeply religious mother, who retains her peasant faith despite the mockings of her husband, who says things like 'She has gone mad, she worships Jesu Messi at the same time as Vishnu, Krishna, the Koran and Tapji'.[11] Anand never scorns the fate of the peasantry, though he can neither intellectually nor emotionally share it, and indeed in another novel, *The Big Heart*, he can appeal with desperation, 'Oh, put some pity in the souls of the people.'[12] Pity, but not faith in God. The portrait that he draws of his mother in these autobiographical novels imbues her with peasant strength and humility. Anand perfectly understands the psychological necessity for her unshakeable, if intellectually confused, religious beliefs. She was betrothed at the age of eight. She exchanged her village home, where she had responsibilities to look after her younger brothers and sisters, for 'the sense of responsibility that had been customary to inoculate into the minds of young brides ... "Be like Savitri" had been her father's blessing, "Be like the suttees of the Gurus. Loyal to your husband unto death."[13] Krishan often hears his mother talking about her early life, and it is through the stories she tells that Krishan/Anand feels his first stirrings of compassion for the poor. Here is a brief piece from *Seven Summers*:

> The domestic atmosphere alone in that world of mud homesteads, built on high plinths, with verandahs and courtyards, clustering together beside the green field, under the silver-white sky, from the milking of cows at early dawn, the churning of curds for butter, the sweeping, the treating of the courtyards with antiseptic cow-dung, the cooking, the serving, the spinning, the weaving, and the washing was an experience so intensely hard, that only the ritualization of it lifted it above the taint of slavery and utter long-drawn monotony and sordidness.[14]

This world of buildings clustering together beside the green fields, under the silver-white sky, with the milking of cows at early dawn and the churning of curds, suggests a pastoral idyll, but we have too the blunt social reality, the taint of slavery and the long-drawn monotony and sordidness. This union of pastoral reminiscence and a kind of humanist assertion that things must change is really what makes up the strength of both *Seven Summers* and *Morning Face*. It is hardly surprising, therefore, that in *Morning Face* we find Krishan, though unable to share his mother's religious faith, emulating her moral strength of purpose. He says, 'I would often go without food in the effort to keep the kind of fast she kept, in order to become immune to hunger, in order to starve, if need be, for revolution.'[15] What we see in the first two novels of the sequence is Krishan's substitution of a humanist faith for a belief in a Muslim, Hindu or a Christian god. When he says toward the end of *Morning Face*, shortly before directing a well-aimed spit at the local temple, 'I felt that I was not only a rebel, but revolt itself',[16] he goes beyond the conventional assertiveness of an angry young man to state the religious doxology and belief that has sustained him throughout his life.

In *Morning Face*, the novel of school days and of adolescence, we are introduced to Indian nationalism. It had first entered Anand's consciousness through his being in Delhi at the time of the Delhi Durbar in 1911 when King George V and Queen Mary were crowned as Emperor and Empress of India, the absolute acme of the Raj. It is during this period that *Morning Face* takes place, and it was during the First World War years that Anand/Krishan first encountered the teachings of Mahatma Gandhi. He was greatly attracted to Gandhi's compassion for the poor, and this is described through very close observation of a number of incidents of human suffering. His attraction toward political nationalism in this period, remembering that Amritsar was the scene of the Dyer massacre in which the British turned on an Indian crowd, profoundly affected Anand. In *The Bubble* Anand moved away from that nationalism, as Krishan encounters alternative beliefs and possibilities in his visit to London.

In attempting to analyze what is at fault in the running of society Anand does not take refuge in mere polemics at the expense of the British Raj, though indictment of colonial rule is one part of his overall perception. The foundation of society in capitalism, which is as much inherent, he argues, in Indian traditional commerce as it is in the superimposition of western ideas, is condemned both in the autobiographical sequence and in the novels that he wrote in the 1940s. It becomes explicit in the two novels of Anand's that are perhaps most admired in the Soviet Union, *The Big Heart*, in which he writes of the coppersmiths, and *Two Leaves in a Bud*. These two novels take a form not unlike that of Soviet socialist realism, which has never been much emulated in western fiction. Money is for Anand a vast impersonal mechanism of power and the inexorable force with which it governs life is to him one of the tragedies of contemporary existence. When Anand says, in a lengthy dedication to *Morning Face*, that money has become to our age what the gods were to previous ages, it is not so much meant that men have found an alternative idol to worship, other than religion, but that money controls and commands life now in the way that the gods were presumed to dictate life in earlier eras. It is as if God had abdicated his authority and handed over to Money. Therefore, Krishan/Anand avers, only in total revolution can there be optimism. In *Confession of a Lover* and *The Bubble* we see some of this romantic radicalism dissipated by the sexual complications of young adulthood and by encounters with many alternative philosophies of life, both political and spiritual. We now meet real historical people as characters in the novels. There are few novelists in the western tradition who have attempted to weave into their works of fiction major protagonists who are actual historical personages. Disraeli is a rare example. In *Confession of a Lover* and in *The Bubble* we encounter such people as the great Urdu poet, Mohammed Iqbal, the British campaigner for Indian rights, Annie Besant, E.M. Forster, the Woolfs, Bertrand Russell, and the nationalist Palm Dutt. Suffering is no longer externalised as something that happens to millions of peasants who can be anonymously pitied; it happens personally and terribly to Krishan himself. It becomes real, rather than intellectualised, through the suicide of his favourite aunt, or through the loss of his loved one Yasmine, in a fruitless Muslim marriage that takes her into purdah and to an early grave. As in Lawrence's *Sons and Lovers* the agonies of sexual awakening are placed alongside the main character's growing interest in the public world. The final words of Anand's *Confession of a Lover* are 'the bright star Venus had appeared overhead', suggesting some prospect of things still to come, the light that he awaits. It carries the same anticipation of a renewed vitality and sense of wonder in the future that Lawrence conveys at the end of *Sons and Lovers*: 'he walked toward the faintly humming glowing town quickly.' At the end of both novels, the hero-protagonist seems to stand at some kind of crossroads where he can either retreat into despair or go forward with all the energy and difficulty of facing up to life. Anand leaves Krishan poised on the discovery of another world, England, with its different culture and equivocal morality.

This world is described in *The Bubble*, an astonishingly vigorous novel. It has an epic panoramic determination to recall across sixty years the events of a Third World person, arriving in London and being taken up in a rather patronising way by the Bloomsbury group. We have a view into Bloomsbury that no one else could possibly supply. Anand's accounts of meetings with such people as Leonard and Virginia Woolf, and with T.S. Eliot, both in this novel and in *Conversations in Bloomsbury* are extraordinarily interesting.

> If I can sense my true feelings, [he writes in a diary entry on 14 November 1925 - I take it that it is an actual diary entry written on that day, just slightly amended to make it relevant to the present day] it is this very contradiction which is perhaps the truth about me just now. I seem to find myself torn between the pulls of two passions. One, to read and read and read and master the philosophical problems posed by various thinkers so that I can have the confidence to understand everything that is being discussed in seminars. [He has arrived as a student at London University where he is studying philosophy.] Two, the urgent and secret desire to write a novel of the quest, like *Portrait of the Artist as a Young Man* by James Joyce. A novel, like Joyce's, but not so abstract. To reconstruct my being by recalling the concrete experiences in which I occasionally became aware of myself in the past. For if words are to mean anything, they must communicate the immediate intimate truth of the self. All those feelings, urges, dreams, fantasies, which come from the labyrinths, and open up the body's soul to the third eye of Shiva. To inspire one to expressions about one's own consciousness and that of others, by comprehension of the totality of circumstances. I would not like to imitate Joyce, because my background has been different, but I'd been fascinated to see, after reading *The Portrait* twice, that the 'I' in the first person singular novel, whom Joyce writes about, assumes different incarnations, through the experiences of

his adolescent years especially when, in his discussions about religion, Stephen Daedalus discovers a conscience in himself. In the end he goes out of Ireland, becomes an exile, to test himself on the smithy of his soul every day. But as his environment is European, and the concrete details of western life are shared between him and his audience, his 'I' becomes the 'we' of the west, almost the Faustian ego trying to take his soul back from Mephistopheles. As a philosopher, I must aspire to be the conscience of my own people. Albeit a bad conscience, as they are sunk in millions of slaveries, from which they have yet to emerge to freedom.[17]

In *The Bubble* there are many pages written like this and critics of Anand's recent work have argued that it should have had a publisher's editor to hack it around, but I feel that if that were done something of the very prolific outpourings of his imagination would be constrained and we would be losing a great deal. In the preface to *Conversations in Bloomsbury*, which seems to run in parallel to *The Bubble*, we have some sense of Anand the man at this interesting period, and of his relationship to western writing.

I arrived in London after a brief gaol-going in the Gandhi movement in the early twenties and found myself removed suddenly from the realities of the freedom struggle, to the world of Bloomsbury, where the pleasures of literature and art were considered ends in themselves. Through such coincidences as frequently happen in a metropolis, I met some members of the legendary Bloomsbury group, Forster, Leonard Woolf, Virginia Woolf, Clive Bell, as well as those who were friendly neighbours, Bonamy Dobree, T.S. Eliot, Arthur Wayley, Berol Dezoit, John Maynard Keynes, and Madame Locacova and the more distant Edwardians, like Lawrence Binyon, and Georgians, D.H. Lawrence, Aldous Huxley, John Middleton Murray, Edith Sitwell and Herbert Read. Also I became part of the lunatic fringe of young literary aspirants who met in the bookshops, pubs and cafes near the British Museum, among whom were the American poet Harold Munro, the Indian dilettante Nikil Sihm, Gwenda Zeitman, later to become well-known as a translator from Italian into English, Nancy Cunard, pioneer of negro consciousness and Catherine Carswell, biographer of the fiery D.H. Lawrence. And while eating sandwiches and feeding pigeons by the corinthian pillars of our Mecca at that time, I made friends with an Australian woman suffragette, Emily Richardson, and the craftsman-sculptor, Eric Dill. In the museum tavern I met Cockney bus drivers and bus conductors, Bill Bland and Harry Thompkins, respectively. I then recorded some of my talks with these writers, which I have since revised. Bloomsbury appears in these conversations to be a much wider area than Virginia Woolf's drawing-room in Tavistock Square. Exuberant, naive poet, hugging Iqbal's *Secret of the Self* under one arm, with the sceptic Hume's treatise facing me on the reading room's desk, I discovered James Joyce's *Portrait of the Artist as a Young Man* with the hero's insistence on going away to 'encounter for the millionth time the reality of experience and to forge in the smithy of my soul the uncreated conscience of my race' and I was inspired to begin a confessional novel of my own.[18]

That confessional novel is *The Bubble* and its predecessors, *Seven Summers, Morning Face* and *Confession of a Lover*. The sequence, still to be completed, is the major *Bildungsroman* of Indian literature, introducing to India a form of fiction which no one else has attempted. If he lives to finish the sequence we shall have a version of the history of India and the history of Anand from approximately 1930 to the present day, when he finds himself on the Sikh hit-list. Anand's prominence in Indian society remains important and I think the Bloomsbury phase will be seen as only a small part of his life. It is a phase, albeit a unique one for an Indian writer. In the full sequence, even if it remains at four, certainly if it goes on to seven, I think that we will have a portrait of contemporary India this century that is unique in scale and in the epic demands that it makes on the reader. 'I realise that in our country there are only two kinds of people; saints and sinners. Those who have changed their minds, those who had no minds to change.' I have no doubt into which category this great and versatile novelist falls.

NOTES

1. Mulk Raj Anand, *Untouchable* (London: Lawrence and Wishart, 1935; Harmondsworth: Penguin, 1986).
2. Mulk Raj Anand, *Two Leaves and a Bud* (London: Lawrence and Wishart, 1937).
3. Mulk Raj Anand, *The King Emperor's English, or The Role of the English Language in the Free India* (Bombay: Hind Kitabs, 1948).
4. Mulk Raj Anand, *Private Life of an Indian Prince* (London: Hutchinson, 1953).
5. Mulk Raj Anand, *Seven Summers: The Story of an Indian Childhood* (London: Hutchinson, 1951).
6. Mulk Raj Anand, *Morning Face* (Bombay: Kutub-Popular, 1968).
7. Mulk Raj Anand, *Confession of a Lover* (New Delhi: Arnold-Heinemann, 1976).
8. Mulk Raj Anand, *The Bubble* (New Delhi: Arnold-Heinemann, 1984).
9. Alastair Niven, *The Yoke of Pity: the Fictional Writings of Mulk Raj Anand* (New Delhi: Arnold-Heinemann, 1978).
10. Mulk Raj Anand, *Conversations in Bloomsbury* (London: Wildwood House, 1981).
11. *Seven Summers*, pp. 121-2.
12. Mulk Raj Anand, *The Big Heart* (London: Hutchinson, 1945), p. 208.
13. *Seven Summers*, p. 69
14. Ibid., p. 68.
15. *Morning Face*, p. 135.
16. Ibid., p. 497.
17. *The Bubble*, p. 78.
18. Preface to *Conversations in Bloomsbury*, pp. 5-6.

AUTHOR'S NOTE

Since this article was completed two further autobiographically based fictions of Mulk Raj Anand have been published. *Pilpali Sahib: The Story of a Big Ego in a Small Body* (London: Aspect, 1990) is the first published version of *My Childhood* which Anand, after suffering a breakdown, sent to Sigmund Freud at the latter's request. *Little Plays of Mahatma Gandhi* (New Delhi: Arnold, 1991) is a series of playlets which form part of the fifth novel in the confessional sequence so far encompassing *Seven Summers*, *Morning Face*, *Confession of a Lover* and *The Bubble*. The full novel is still being completed and will be entitled *And So He Plays His Part*.

Peter Porter

FAST FORWARD

The view from Patmos, the ghost inside
the module! Living neither long enough
nor so curtly brings us nominative snakes,
time turned to blood upon the hour,
fours and sevens when the Lamb lies down
with Fury. And then Sir Headlong tells us
he has tripped and toiled along a donkey path,
the scala of so many angels, with a guide
who features in the brochures: old white hopes
that flavour an apocalypse, aunties
of the terrible abstractions, all made decent
when the fire has crept into a governed switch.

Now it is remaindered into visions,
into the history of the race, fast forward,
the tape so stretched it might at any second
snap to oblivion. And they understood,
those heavy visionaries on poles
or sorting through the dung of lions,
that the countenance of state,
rock-featured and as bright as Caesar's eyes,
floats on insane shoulders. The boat for Patmos
is never late and though the island's rainfall's

doubtful its climate is compact despair,
angels in uniform identified on land.

Sitting with a little health-food lunch
among the flowers of a military estate
we have to calm ourselves by crooning
death songs to the mush of midday heat.
Left to itself, the brain, circuiting the world,
becomes a rapid deployment force
and blasts ashore on any troubled sand.
Where will the end be staged, and whose hand,
held against the light, shall glow brighter
than a thousand suns? Helicoptering
in lightning numbers, the god of prose
hears his own voice prophesying peace.

CITIES OF LIGHT

Here where as yet the minor monsters rove,
Yellow hats and orange jackets and
Theodolited stick-insects on tufts
Of spear-grass, our great ancestors put
One of their stations of the god of dreams,
Well-known to them as this bus-stop to you –
You cannot see it, though it's palpable.

And so with feral cats (a silly name
For constant friends) and tins and saucepans where
The sparrows and the mynahs splash, and dogs
That take what well-fed dogs refuse, we squat,
A hamlet of the harmless and the mad,
Defying parliament, that bank of acts,
Stung by the dew when Autumn tents us down.

The cops will come: this is a decent land,
So here injustice calls for little force
And fewer still will see it happening.
We can no longer hope for help from those
Who set the stars upon the pegs of night,
For they have gone away. But let none think
This metal world is newer than our own.

Ours was the great renunciation; we
Gave up everything that jumps and sparks
And flies. The curious who come to nose
At us will never leave the murderous weald
Of bulldozers, their kitchen-teatowel world
Of planted trees. They've sold their spirits to
Half-angels of some immortality.

The kind that speaks of progress and runs through
Every sacred thing like strings of fire,
In passage showing how a land may die.
Men do not live the longer and the rose
Will service them for graves as well as hearths.
Our people had these tools, our myths were mad.
We shrugged them off, we learned to live by light.

We took technology and turned it in
Upon itself – the grand computers learned
That trees had memory banks, that pollen was
A pure retrieval system and when ants
Assembled city states diplomacy
Attained a grace which even schools of night
Might envy, seeking Martian metaphors.

Our learning told us that the gods came down
Not to impose their rule on croft and creek
But to take holidays away from dark
In this domain more beautiful than theirs,
And like all tourists to seem out of place,

A nuisance to the locals, but with power
To make or mar their taut economy.

After repudiation came the dreams!
We drifted back to such complexity
Our daily actions seemed slow-motion rides.
When we were found by later schematists,
We looked in outward far from what we were,
Old Primitives, mere gatherers, un-wheeled,
Becalmed by symbols, unconcerned by time.

Our cities were invisible to them
And always will be while their eyes unhorse
Reality with expectation. This site,
Where even now the sub-contractors start
To plan their glass and galvanising push,
Was never one of our more sterling forts,
A mere sub-station on the grid of dreams.

But worth defending. When they move us on
Their blindness will increase. One day perhaps
Their quondam cities filed away in squares
Will show our country's faces to the moon
Enacting open nothing to despair
And each surveying colonel will be hauled
Down from his statue in the seasoned park.

And then the true, the cities made of light,
Which once we had and which we gave away
Will come into their own. Already they
Are blazing in the night. Your astronauts
High-riding on Australia see their glow
And look at maps and read just emptiness
Outshining all the rules of blood and steel.

STICKING TO THE TEXT

In the Great Book of Beginning we read
That the word was God and was with God
And are betrayed by the tiniest seed
Of all the world's beginnings, to thrash,
Like sprats in a bucket, caught in deed
As in essence by shapes of ourselves,
Our sounds the only bargains we may plead.

So starts this solipsistic essay about words,
Its first stanza chasing its own tail,
Since no word will betray another word
In this sodality, self-repressing and male,
And we discover, hardly believing our eyes
And ears, a sort of chromatic scale,
That whatever lives and feels is logos.

Tell us then, vanity, what is truth
And how does it differ from honesty?
Ecclesiastics and analysts play sleuth
To that slippery murderer, but they require
The rack and the couch, tell the story of Ruth
Out of her country, such cheats of championship
As the Noble Savage or General Booth.

We can know only what words may say
Though we may say what we know is untrue.
Honesty lines up its troops – Thersites,
Iago, Tartuffe, The New York Review –
The confessional rolls, the lottery pays
Timely prizes to me and to you,
Truly honest people, tied to the wheel.

And when love announces it is here
Either with a lily and spasm of light

Or rising from a childhood bed of fear
To assume its pilgrimage of grace,
It brings its style wars and its gear,
The triolets of touch, the ribboned letters,
Pictures of annus mirabilis or just last year.

Keeping ahead of death and Deconstruction
We have the text we need to play the game,
But what should we do to make it personal –
Your text, my text – are they the same?
The rules are on the inside of the lid
As fate appoints its contestants and fame
Picks one from the Great House and one from the Pale.

Too many fortunes are made by the Absurd:
It's better to run in the linear race
Where everything connects which has occurred,
Better to suffer the nightmares natural to
The body and tell what you have heard
Among your fellow sufferers and hope
The story's end won't choke you on a word.

Some Outstanding
Australian Poets Today

PETER PORTER

Perhaps the gloomiest way to look at poetry is to recognize that it is hardly a spectator sport. Those who write it sometimes read it: hardly anyone else does. Yet, in every society I have any experience of, poetry is being written in ever-increasing quantities. In part this is because a poem is one of the few artistic forms which enables its creator to conceive and execute a work in one span of concentration. (I do not assert, of course, that all poems are written that way: some may be worried over like crocheting or embroidery.) But each country's poetry does not necessarily command the respect or even the attention of every other country. I don't worry about this myself, since I agree with W.H. Auden, who wrote that a poet's hope was to be 'like some valley cheese,/ local, but prized elsewhere'. To simplify grossly, you could say that poetry in English was dominated by poetry *written in England* until sometime around the beginning of the Nineteen Twenties. Even after that, with Eliot and Pound writing in Europe, and Wallace Stevens hardly known beyond America's shores, the British hegemony persisted. It is almost dead today, but I believe that it has been replaced largely and even more brutally by the dominance of the United States. (In passing, I should like to make it plain that I do not refer to the political supremacy of the U.S. when I speak of such a dominance. Gertrude Stein said that America was the oldest country of the twentieth century. The United States also pioneered every style and system whereby we, in the West and even the majority of people in the Third World, live and know ourselves – marketing, popular entertainment, language, production-line tooling-up, the whole parcel of contemporary methodology and self-awareness.) It is true that the deep past still stems from Britain – the great classics of English literature are not American in essence though U.S. scholarship has imperialised them. It is a characteristic American ploy to imply that the Europeans, and particularly the English, are sloppy and inadequate guardians of their own inheritance. This is not so brutal a takeover bid as it may seem. Shakespeare, for instance, is as close to the citizens of Kalamazoo, Kalgoorlie, and Kimberly as he is to the descendents of his contemporaries in Kidderminster.

I have devoted so much time to this preamble since I feel from what has been said at this conference already, and I prophesy will go on being the case, that America and American literature will be the King Charles's Head of a conference concerned with Commonwealth literature. Commonwealth countries can define themselves with regard to Britain itself, or to each other, or to non-Anglophone third-world countries, or to Europe in its post-imperial phase. They can proudly affirm a continuing if previously overlaid tradition or they may choose to see a tense but invigorating future for their cultures – but, alas, what they usually don't like doing is recognizing that, along with European societies and the resented British motherland, they are all satellites of the culture of the United States. None more clearly so than Australia.

Having pointed to Australia's unawareness of American cultural imperialism while being hypersensitive to the British sort, I shall go ahead to contradict myself by stating that the production of poetry in Australia today is at a level the equal of that in Britain and (give or take a few mighty names) the U.S. This may be saying no more than that all contemporary poets writing in English inhabit a world of Post-Modernism. Experiment is not over, but it tends to be conducted by individual talents in pursuit of personal solutions. The modern poet, in Australia as elsewhere, enters the permanent museum, which is his artistic inheritance, and tries to find the best way to express his own destiny using the vernacular he was born speaking and the classical precedents he discovers for himself. The word vernacular allows me to introduce one of the most important names in contemporary Australian poetry – that of Les A. Murray. Murray has a genius for titles, and the one he chose for his collected volume of poems was *The Vernacular Republic*. Murray is a democrat but a democrat with a difference. Vernacular to him means more than just the everyday and the demotic. It stands for a consciously Australian idiom, one gathering the best of public and private speech as used by his fellow-countrymen, but also the harvest of literary invention possible from the many Englishes of our far-flung linguistic empire. Murray is didactic in that he believes that Australia is, in a quite unironic sense, 'the lucky country'. Previous authors, including the originator of the phrase 'lucky country' (Donald Horne), have chosen to emphasise Australia's unwillingness to appreciate that its good living and economic tolerance spring from fortunate circumstances of geography and history. Murray believes rather that they are an expression of the genius of the people, and that any tendency to praise Nature in Australia at the expense of the humans who live in its midst is snobbery. Not for him that aristocratic disdain for the people of Australia mixed with appreciation of the continent's pantheistic spirit, which will be found in the writings and utterances of both Randolph Stow and Patrick White. I find Murray perfectly realistic in this. Nature in Australia does indeed have a monumental quality, an indifference to human will. A

ormed landscape owing its lineaments to the shaping
hand of inventive man, of which perhaps the topography
of England is the finest example to be found anywhere, is
impossible in Australia. But this does not mean that
Nature alone is a true subject for poetry in Australia since
it possesses the only available grandeur. Les Murray has
hit on the important theme of human redemption (it is not
surprising that Murray is a Catholic by conversion). What
began under the auspices of Hell – the First Fleet and the
convict colony at Sydney Cove – has blossomed into a new
democracy, free of hopelessness in the European sense, but
not, of course, untouched by original sin. One of Murray's
characteristic phrases speaks of 'Europe's socialist misère'.
Murray is not so naive as to think that people are bound
to be happy in Australia. But he does believe that Australia could be the home of a redeemed species, a people
instinctively democratic who will be helped by a provident
nature to live their lives productively. To this end, too, he
welcomes anyone to his vernacular republic, especially
those who are not Anglo-Saxon and are untainted by the
colonial dependence which he detests. One of his collections of poems is entitled *Ethnic Radio*, and he brings to all
his verse a pentecostal gift of tongues. His most recent
poems show him coping with machines, those signs of
today which most poets simply ignore, trusting only their
beloved versions of pastoral. His just published collection,
The People's Otherworld, includes poems with titles such as
'The Sydney Highrise Variations', 'The Quality of Sprawl'
and 'Machine Portraits with Pendant Spacemen'. But
Murray is still recognizably in the central Australian literary tradition – of bush apostolic descent. I have only
space and time to quote two passages from him – one to
represent the eloquent baroque language with which he
clothes perfectly familiar Australian country images, and
the other his equally effective way with laconics (the word
itself the title of one of his most passionate evocations of
the love of the land which pervades Bush bucolics).

Ideally, of course, Australians seeking a past pantheon of verse to celebrate should look back to Chaucer and Wordsworth. These are the makers of the language they use. But those poets were Englishmen, and nationalists have tried instead to impress the Aboriginal legends (not of course the Aboriginal language) into service as proper Australian myth material. Such attempts have been pretty unsuccessful, with the exception of Murray's extended long-lined sequence known as 'The Buledelah-Taree Holiday Song Cycle'. In this Murray takes the intensely nominative and litanic method of Aboriginal poem-chant as his means of celebrating the new owners of the sacred land – the farmers and holiday-makers of the dairy and timber country along the coast north of Sydney in New South Wales. There is nothing at all left of the Aboriginal material – it is the method only which has been adopted. Murray thus escapes the deadening 'Hiawatha' effect which often results when Europeans think themselves into utterly different traditions. The following quotation is just one of several sections of the poem.

> Now the sun is an apple-green blindness through the
>   swells, a white blast on the sea-face, flaking and shoaling;
> now it is burning off the mist; it is emptying the density
>   of trees, it is spreading upriver,
> hovering above the casuarina needles, there at Old Bar and
>   Manning Point;
> flooding the island farms, it abolishes the milkers'
>   munching breath
> as they walk towards the cowyards; it stings a bucket here
>   a teacup there.
> Morning steps into the world by ever more southerly
>   gates; shadows weaken their north skew
> on Middle Brother, on Cape Hawke, on the dune scrub
>   toward Seal Rocks;
> steadily the heat is coming on, the butter-water time, the
>   clothes-sticking time;
> grass covers itself with straw; abandoned things are
>   thronged with spirits;

everywhere wood is still with strain; birds hiding down
  the creek galleries, and in the cockspur canes;
the cicada is hanging up her sheets; she takes wing off her
  music-sheets.
Cars pass with a rational zoom, panning quickly towards
  Wingham,
through the thronged and glittering, the shale-topped
  ridges, and the cattlecamps,
towards Wingham for the cricket, the ball knocked hard
  in front of smoked-glass ranges, and for the drinking.
In the time of heat, the time of flies around the mouth,
  the time of the west verandah;
looking at that umbrage along the ranges, on the New
  England side;
clouds begin assembling vaguely, a hot soiled heaviness on
  the sky, away there towards Gloucester;
a swelling up of clouds, growing there above Mount
  George, and above Tipperary;
far away and hot with light; sometimes a storm takes root
  there, and fills the heavens rapidly;
darkening, boiling up and swaying on its stalks, pulling this
  way and that, blowing round by Krambach;
coming white on Bulby, it drenches down on the paddocks
  and on the white fences;
the paddocks are full of ghosts, and people in cornbag
  hoods approaching;
lights are lit in the house; the storm veers mightily on its
  stem, above the roof; the hills uphold it;
the stony hills guide its dissolution; gullies opening and
  crumbling down, wrenching tussocks and rolling them;
the storm carries a greenish-grey bag; perhaps it will find
  hail and send it down, starring cars, flattening tomatoes,
in the time of the Washaways, of the dead trunks braiding
  water, and of the Hailstone Yarns.

Perhaps truer to the inhabitants of his Australia Felix is
Murray's short poem 'Rainwater Tank'. Despite the picnics,
the national parks, the barbecue sites and the mineral
boom, Australians have always had a hard struggle to
wrest a living from the land. There is another side to their
hedonism, a more enduring and stoical approach to nature.
In a land where drought is the general and not the

unusual experience, the galvanised iron-ringed tank fo
storing rainwater is more than a symbol, it is a lifeline i
itself. Alas, for so many small farmers, the line runs lik
a noose to the local bank and its habit of foreclosing o
debtors. All this is exquisitely delineated in Murray'
poem.

> Empty rings when tapped give tongue,
> rings that are tense with water talk:
> as he sounds them, ring by rung,
> Joe Mitchell's reddened knuckles walk.
>
> The cattledog's head sinks down a notch
> and another notch, beside the tank,
> and Mitchell's boy, with an old jack-plane,
> lifts moustaches from a plank.
>
> From the puddle that the tank has dripped
> hens peck glimmerings and uptilt
> their heads to shape the quickness down;
> petunias live on what gets spilt.
>
> The tankstand spider adds a spittle
> thread to her portrait of her soul.
> Pencil-grey and stacked like shillings
> out of a banker's paper roll
>
> stands the tank, roof-water drinker.
> The downpipe stares drought into it.
> Briefly the kitchen tap turns on
> then off. But the tank says Debit, Debit.

Opposed to Murray, yet in many ways admiring him,
are the several schools of Modernists who look variously
to America and the European avant-garde for their inspiration. One must remember that these days a fashion is no
sooner born somewhere than it may be taken up anywhere
else. There is no longer a time-gap in sophistication – that
particularly Australian form of debilitation (cause of the
horrible phrase 'the cultural cringe') named by Geoffrey
Blainey, 'the tyranny of distance'. So, on the one hand a

group of enthusiasts in Sydney translates the latest musings by the French literary theorists even before London and New York know of them. On the other, good and audacious poets in Sydney and Melbourne are so familiar with the American poetry scene that they can handle the heady enthusiasms of New York, San Francisco or the Mid-West without losing their own identity. Naming names is like picking teams – not everyone will be happy in the uniform you give him – but it is perhaps not too much of a simplification to say that John Tranter stands at the head of experiment in Australian verse, as Les Murray does in what I can only call 'poetry of consolidation'. One of Murray's keenest followers, however, Robert Gray, is perhaps the most knowledgeable poet in Australia, knowing quite as much about American styles as anyone in Tranter's camp. Gray knows many other less widely developed styles as well – for instance, he is as likely to look to Francis Ponge as to John Ashbery. Tranter set out to break the ring of the older poets, what one might call the academic ascendency and the bush hegemony. At present, his followers include John Forbes, Martin Johnstone, Laurie Duggan, John Scott and, at various places on the fringe, loners such as Alan Wearne. Young writers like Gig Ryan look to him too. He is a good standard-bearer and polemicist. Rather more important, Tranter is a fine poet in his own right. He belongs, however much he may repudiate the immediate Australian past, in a strong native tradition of the urban, the colloquial, the sardonic and polemic. Reading Rimbaud may have started his quest for Modernity, but he is more firmly rooted in the myths and traditions of Sydney life than any other poet working in Australia. In this he resembles such fiercely demotic figures as Bruce Dawe, of Melbourne and Toowoomba, a fine vernacular poet who owes no allegiance to any school of literature, a writer whose utterance is *sui generis*, rising out of the cadences and vocabulary of Australian speech. John Forbes admires the playful New Yorkers, especially Frank

O'Hara. His poetry is perhaps the most original in Australia at present and also, interestingly, the most redolent of the Australian way of looking at the world. It is a measure of Australia's present-day maturity that it has its own manner of being avant-garde. Hero worship of the great Modernists no longer leads to mere sedulousness or the suppression of idiosyncracy. In a short talk like this one, I can afford to quote only one more poem, and I have chosen a light but characteristic one by Tranter, 'Speakeasy'. At first it may strike you as rather American. A satire on a wheeler-dealer, politician, one of the endlessly opportunistic exploiters who come to the surface in any democratic mercantile society. But it is deeply Australian in its combination of lightly malicious observation and corner-of-the-mouth demotic. Underneath, Tranter is serious. He has his own ideas of Australia as the good land, though they are not the same as Les Murray's.

> We've checked out the story and it's true –
> he was once an overweight philosopher
> dizzy with food and fond of spankings,
> then he got tamed and rich, in that order,
> then he entered politics and made a killing.
> Like a painted model of a car he spoke fluently
> but his promises writhed under a net.
> What he said became a mass market,
> his words are diagrams of sickness
> buried in pornography and power graphs,
> and he thinks in sub-titles no one
> can read fast enough. Don't think his tears
> are make-up, they come from a wrecked future
> that ends in a million years of darkness,
> like yours and mine. His dreams,
> at their worst, are not made of images
> but a kind of verbal damage. Is he the Poet
> we keep asking for, or the one we keep feeding?
> Or the one we need? Make it easy,
> he begged us, make it easy for me,
> idealism is a language I understand,
> offer me a deal. My lips are sealed,
> he said, then he told us everything.

I have not traced the central tradition in Australian poetry, only called it up to give a locus in which to place the poets I have spoken about. The anti-Modernism of A.D. Hope and James McAuley; the political poets of Melbourne and Adelaide; the brilliant generation of Melbourne University poets, which includes Evan Jones, Chris Wallace-Crabbe and Vincent Buckley, and which might be thought of as a 'school of Auden'; the Sydney bohemians, Robert Adamson and Nigel Roberts, close to but not entirely sympathetic to Tranter and his group; the conservationists best epitomised in Judith Wright – these are just a few of the groupings I have left undescribed. I leave you though with one observation which will go far to illustrate how busy the poetry world of Australia is. No country has produced, in recent years, so many different contemporary anthologies of poetry. They are combative or inclusive or decorative or narrowly didactic – they come in every sort. And, for someone who has lived most of his life outside his native land, as I have, the poems they include reveal something which I suspect is not so readily seen in Australia itself – avant or arrière garde, the finest Australian poems have a flavour which will not be found in any other literature written in English. There is now a common tone as well as a common inheritance. You can say it is thoroughly Australian.

Miles Franklin:
The Outside Track*

ANNA RUTHERFORD

> PRESERVATION OF THINGS MOST PRECIOUS TO THE
> HUMAN SOUL SOMETIMES LIES IN RENUNCIATION
>
> Miles Franklin, Prelude to Waking

> *Oh girls, girls*
> *Silly little valuable things*
> *You should have said, No, I am valuable*
> *And again, It is because I am valuable*
> *I say, No.*
>
> Stevie Smith

> You will marvel at the labour that ended in so little but what
> you will never know is how it was thinking of you and for you,
> that we struggled as we did and accomplished the little which
> we have done; that it was in the thought of your larger
> realisation and fuller life, that we found consolation for the
> futilities of our own.
>
> Olive Schreiner, Woman and Labour

The occasion which prompted this paper was a remark
made at the Commonwealth Women Writers' seminar and
workshop held in London at the Commonwealth Institute.
One of the texts chosen for discussion was Miles Franklin's
My Brilliant Career. The film version of the book was also
shown. At the end of the day the discussion leader was

asked to sum up the conclusions which had been reached. And my ears pricked up when I heard her say that the one thing they could all agree upon was that the heroine of the film was a much nicer person that the heroine of the book. I would like to examine briefly this statement before turning to the major issue with which I wish to deal.

It is fairly easy to account for the technical superiority of the film over the novel. Its director, Gillian Armstrong, has all the advantages of living and working in a feminist milieu; Miles Franklin suffered all the disadvantages that Elaine Showalter discusses in *A Literature of Their Own*[1] and which Frances McInherny deals with in her article 'Miles Franklin, *My Brilliant Career* and *The Female Tradition*'.[2] Whilst I don't think that Frances McInherny regards Australian literature as a second-class relative of English literature, I do agree with Delys Bird[3] that more can be gained by directing one's inquiry and criticism towards an aesthetic of Australian women's fiction. If one does this one can see that Miles Franklin's problems were exacerbated by the male-dominated, anti-intellectual nature of Australian society, and that many of the contradictions and confusions, both in her life and work, were not caused by her own inadequacies but by the nature of the society into which she was born.

To turn again to the film. Like Cassandra Pybus, I recognize that the film maker is within 'her rights to impose romanticised feminist gloss on an admittedly flawed turn of the century adolescent novel'.[4] My contention, however, is that both the heroine of the novel and the woman who wrote it have been cheated in the process. If I can give several brief examples of how the film cheats. Take for instance the opening and closing scenes of the movie. It begins with Sybylla sitting indoors, her notebook on her lap, about to commence her novel. She has already chosen a title, *My Career*, which she writes slowly and deliberately. Having done this she looks up, pauses, then smiling, chuckling almost, she inserts *Brilliant* between *My* and *Career*. The audience response is immediately positive. We too chuckle, and from that moment we are on Sybylla's side. To make absolutely certain of our sympathies, the film director is careful to juxtapose this scene with an outdoor one showing a harsh landscape and men and women struggling in it. It is against odds such as these that Sybylla must fight for her right to be independent, and an artist, but from this opening scene we are never in doubt that she will triumph. The final scene confirms this belief. It shows Sybylla strong and alone in the landscape; the world of Possum Gully is behind her and she gazes confidently into the future. To make absolutely sure we get the message, the publication details of *My Brilliant Career* are superimposed on this image, making us feel that she has achieved what she wanted and whatever sacrifices she might have made have been worth it.

It's a splendid feminist version, it's what we want to happen, but unfortunately it's not true, it's a vision rather than a reality. Not surprisingly, the feminist press have cashed in on the film by using photos from it for the covers of their editions of *My Brilliant Career*.[5] The photo chosen by Virago for their edition is, like most of their covers, particularly appropriate – a defiant Judy Davies (the Australian actress who plays the role of Sybylla) dominates an otherwise empty landscape and defies taming in the same way as her hair does. By placing a still from the film on the cover of the book they are asking us to identify the heroine of the film with that of the book and in turn, in their introduction, they are asking us to identify the heroine with the author.

The Sybylla of the film is, like most of Miles Franklin's heroines, strong-willed, intelligent, questioning and angry about the roles assigned to women. Men are attracted to her, she flirts with them as any normal girl might but refuses to marry them. She is also egoistical, self-centred and selfish. But we are made to understand that these are 'qualities' she needs if she is to triumph (and we want her to triumph). What the film makers are guilty of is the sin of omission. They have left out the question mark from the original title of the book, which was not *My Career* with the later addition of 'Brilliant' as we see it in the film, but *My Brilliant? Career*. It was the publishers, Blackwoods, who removed the question mark. But even though they might remove the question mark from the title they were unable to remove it, and all that it stood for (bitterness, irony, self-doubt, despair) from the book.

The issues, I believe, were far more complex than the film suggests. It's good to applaud the heroine of the film but we should also keep before our eyes what price Miles Franklin paid to have the opinions she had and to lead the life she chose to live. Brought up in a conventional household, proper almost to the point of prudishness, it must have cost her a great deal to go against the norm, particularly in a society that perhaps more than most, believes that 'no one's different without they have something wrong with them'.[6] If suggesting that women were the slaves of men, mere appendages, chattels to be bought and sold on the marriage market was abnormal, she would be willing to accept the tag. What she would shrink from is the notion that she herself was abnormal and that her rejection of marriage had deeper implications. To some male egos it is inconceivable that women might reject them. To such people rejection can only be a sign of abnormality. This attitude is epitomized by Colin Roderick in his biography of Miles Franklin.[7] I can think of few persons less suitable to be her biographer. A brief summary of Roderick's attitude to this subject will show why I hold that opinion.

Roderick would have us believe that Miles's railing against the world and the injustices which she perceived in it had two causes. The first was, according to him, her so-called physical unattractiveness. Here he lays special emphasis on her nose, 'a mere blob on flat features' (p. 67)

121

telling us that whilst her sister had the profile of Helen of Troy, Miles had 'that of a Hottentot' (p. 70) thereby adding racism to his sexism. The other cause, he believes, was due to what he sees as her sexual inadequacy/repression/deviation. Hers was 'a mind smarting under the *delusion* (my emphasis) of sexual discrimination' (p. 134). One is not at all surprised to find Roderick taking up the Havelock Ellis line of thinking. The latter was in Australia when *My Brilliant Career* was published. He wrote a review of it commenting on its bitter and egotistical mood and used it in his lectures as an example of unconscious abnormality. So does Roderick. Any deviation from the norm – his norm – he attributes to sexual inversion. His solution/cure? for Miles Franklin was the usual male chauvinist one. He laments the fact that one of Miles's suitors, her cousin Edwin, 'was no Petruccio', for he believes that 'what she really wanted – and needed – was a masterful reaction' (p. 70). According to Roderick, Miles Franklin was unable to resolve these conflicts within herself and so she, like her heroine, Sybylla, 'made a virtue out of a necessity and decided to be an old maid' (p. 91), to embark on a career, and to leave Australia. Roderick likens Miles's departure to that of 'a bewildered dog that has barked at his master in error, [and then wants] to crawl under cover' (p. 106).

His attitude to her future activities and her writing is, needless to say, predictable. Miles, he tells us, had taken 'the wrong track'. Her 'pursuit of the rainbow was to lead her into a quagmire of irrelevant and wasteful New Woman militancy' (p. 73). 'She spent the best years of her life as lackey to dominating women who were natural obsessed feminists' (p. 73). Not only would he have us believe that her writing reflected her sexual inversion, but the way in which she wrote was also evidence of it. 'Her style mirrored her inverted sexuality. For fidelity to the idiom of literary creation she substituted the catch-cries and slogans of her self-imposed suffragette exile' (p. 73). One wonders if he believes that all suffragettes and feminsts were/are 'sexually inverted'. He probably does. Reading Roderick's book one can only remark on the truth of Shirley Hazzard's statement that 'misogyny is part of the Australian wound'.[8]

I would like to address myself to some of Colin Roderick's remarks. In particular, I would like to take up Miles Franklin's decision to remain single and her attitude to sex and marriage. I am well aware that we all read into a text what we want to read; compare, for instance, the preface written by Henry Lawson for the first edition in 1901 and Carmen Callil's introduction to the Virago edition in 1980. And so I will preface the following remarks with Virginia Woolf's words from *A Room of One's Own*. Woolf writes:

> When a subject is highly controversial – and any question about sex is that – one cannot hope to tell the truth. One can only show how one came to hold whatever opinion one does hold. One can only give one's audience the chance of drawing their own conclusions as they observe the limitations, the prejudices, the idiosyncracies of the speaker.[9]

With that warning I will proceed.

Miles Franklin may have been a rebel in many respects but when it came to matters of sexual morality she clung tenaciously to her respectability and there can be no doubt that she was stung by Havelock Ellis's remarks, indeed some attribute to these remarks her refusal to let *My Brilliant Career* be reprinted – it was over sixty years before it was to be reissued. I would like to look more closely at its sequel, *My Career Goes Bung*.[10] This novel, as far as we know, was written in 1902 but not published until 1946, earlier publishers refusing it on the grounds that it was too outspoken and could contain libellous material. It was interesting to hear Richard Walsh, who at the time was manager of Angus and Robertson, refer to it in a paper he gave at the Australian literature conference at the University of New England, in 1985, as 'that spiteful, little novel'. Old prejudices die hard, it would seem.

We know that one of her reasons for writing *My Career Goes Bung* was to pacify the people who felt they had been maligned in *My Brilliant Career*. But more importantly I believe it was written to refute what she refers to in the introduction as 'those dubious guesses of psychoanalysis' (*My Career Goes Bung*, p. 7) and to state more clearly and openly her ideas about woman's estate. I realize that it is a work of fiction but Miles Franklin herself spoke of 'that truth which is clearer in fiction than in fact'.[11] In the following section I would like to look more closely at some of the issues she raises. I should add that the fact that I make more detailed reference to *My Career Goes Bung* than to *My Brilliant Career* does not mean that I agree with Colin Roderick that in the latter book Franklin failed to bring 'forward any convincing support for Sybylla's decision' not to marry Harry (p. 71). Such a suggestion is ludicrous.

My Career Goes Bung is a fierce denunciation of a society organized in such a way that to be female automatically means that one is inferior. In it Miles Franklin examines society's attitude to women, what is expected of them (what is natural) and what they in turn might expect out of life. The outlook is grim, both for those who conform, and those who fail to do so.

What is woman's natural role? To act as an appendage to the man (her subservient state is natural to her gender), any status she might acquire is by courtesy of the man; 'marriage gives a woman standing,' Henry tells Sybylla, 'lots more standing than sour old school teachers and these other old maids, on their own can have' (*My Career Goes Bung*, p. 224). It should be pointed out that at that time if one was a woman and a school teacher one was also automatically a spinster. The Department of Education required that any woman who married must leave the service, a rule that was in existence long after Miles Franklin wrote this novel.[12]

The married woman's duty was to bear her husband's children, preferably boys, so that his line could be continued and, should he be a poor farmer, to provide him with a free work force. Not surprisingly, patriarchal society was quick to bring in God in support of their position – after all wasn't he a man, too? That they knew an ally when they saw one is reflected in Edmée's statement to Sybylla, 'men say a girl without religion is like a rose without perfume' (*My Career Goes Bung*, p. 139). If the men recognized an ally, Sybylla just as quickly recognized an enemy. The God men invoked was a 'God made by disagreeable and selfish old men in their own image and erected as a bogey to control women' (*My Career Goes Bung*, p. 47). Should the woman object to her role of 'work ox and brood sow' (ten, eleven or twelve children were not unusual), she would be told that this was God's will. It would appear, Sybylla retorted, that God's will and the rabbits coincided.

As so often happens, God and Country were enlisted as joint allies in support of the male position. Arguing for non-interference with the birth rate Father O'Toole tells Sybylla that 'we must fill up Australia and hold it from the Yellow Peril at our doors' (*My Career Goes Bung*, p. 67). Sybylla points out that he himself is not doing anything to help increase the population and goes on to suggest 'that the unfortunate Yellow Peril women might be relieved to enter into an alliance with [the Australian women] to stem the swarming business' (*My Career Goes Bung*, p. 67). This was an interesting reply in the light of Miles Franklin's attitude to nationalism. She was fiercely nationalistic and also supportive of the racism built into Australia's nationalism. On this occasion, however, it seems that her feminism took precedence over both her nationalism and her racism.

Sybylla points out the contradiction between men's belief in their own superiority and the way they react, should they suspect a woman to be intelligent.

> I never can understand why men are so terrified of women hav-
> ing special talents. They have no consistency in argument. They
> are as sure as the rock of Gibraltar that they have all the mental
> superiority and that women are weak-minded, feeble conies; then
> why do they get in such a mad-bull panic at any attempt on the
> part of women to express themselves.
>
> (*My Career Goes Bung*, pp. 128-29)

Like so many issues raised by Miles Franklin, this is one
that George Eliot had taken up in *Middlemarch*. Throughout
this novel, whenever the male/female relationship is discussed and the male assumes a patriarchal attitude, a note
of irony creeps in. Take, for instance, the occasion when
Dorothea makes an impassioned plea to her uncle to see
how incongruous and hypocritical it would be for him to
stand as a Reform candidate for Parliament when conditions on his own estate were so appalling. Will Ladislaw
is also present and we read: 'Will's admiration was accompanied with a chilling sense of remoteness. A man is sel-
dom ashamed of feeling he cannot love a woman so well
when he sees a certain greatness in her; nature having intended greatness for men.' But George Eliot goes on to remark: 'Nature has sometimes made sad oversights in carrying out her intentions.'[13] Just in case there has been some
oversight, men make sure of their own safe position
through the education they make available to women, an
education described by George Eliot as 'that toy-box history of the world adapted to young ladies' (p. 112), so that
women, no matter how intelligent they might be, will be
disadvantaged. As Sybylla points out:

> In the matter of women's brain power they organise conditions
> comparable to a foot race in which they have all the training and
> the proper shoes and little running pants, while women are taken
> out of the plough, so to speak, with harness and winkers still on
> them and are lucky if they are allowed to start at scratch.
>
> (*My Career Goes Bung*, p. 129)

Should the woman persist in her foolish ambitions, the male responds to her challenge/threat by turning her into a figure of ridicule, an unnatural creature. 'A woman with brains,' Sybylla is told, 'is a monstrosity' (*My Career Goes Bung*, p. 128), whilst a woman who writes is likened to a performing bear and, what is more, 'the bear's performance [is] more natural' (*My Career Goes Bung*, p. 128). Scribbling should be left to men and to those women who couldn't catch a man' (*My Career Goes Bung*, p. 124) with the insinuation that women choose a career because no man will choose them. Compare this with Colin Roderick's remarks quoted earlier.[14]

Miles Franklin also exposes men's double standard with regard to 'good' and 'bad' women. Whilst in America she edited with Alice Henry, the feminist, radical journal *Life and Labor*. Sex rarely entered into the pages of this journal, but when it did, it was to point out the male double standard that lay behind prostitution and the white slave trade. There was no suggestion that the moral standard for women be relaxed or changed, rather that men should follow the same standard as they demanded of their 'good' women. They were in line here with the social purity feminists like Christabel Pankhurst who demanded 'Votes for Women, Chastity for Men'.

The same views are expressed in *My Career Goes Bung*. Sybylla condemns the double standard of men who frequent the brothel and at the same time demand that the women they marry be virgins. She exposes would-be seducers like Hardy who looked upon women as being created solely for the delights of men, and, with a touch worthy of George Eliot, points out that even if such a man has more knowledge of the world, 'a woman has the advantage if she is equally matched in intelligence ... for she has depths that he does not suspect because some of them he will not concede to her' (*My Career Goes Bung*, p. 187).[15]

Let us look more closely at some of the implications of Miles Franklin's situation. Much has been made of her heroines' aversion to sex and indeed of her own aversion. Some male critics have been quick to point out that her fondness for horses and being photographed with a riding crop or an umbrella was simply a manifestation of her penis envy. She was aware of this and refuted it through her heroine: 'Never in my life had I a wish to be a man. Such a suggestion fills me with revulsion. What I raged against were the artificial restrictions' (*My Career Goes Bung*, p. 16). Compare the like reaction of a much more recent fictional heroine whose situation and ambitions were in many ways similar to that of Sybylla. I am referring to Dell, the heroine of Alice Munro's *Lives of Girls and Women*: 'Everything from advertisements to F. Scott Fitzgerald to a frightening song on the radio *"the girl that I marry will have to be as soft and as pink as a nursery"* was urging, telling Dell to be something that she was not.'[16] She reads an article in one of the magazines on the subject of the basic difference between the male and female habits of thought:

> The author was a famous New York psychiatrist, a disciple of Freud. He said that the difference between the male and female modes of thought were easily illustrated by the thoughts of a boy and girl, sitting on a park bench, looking at the full moon. The boy thinks of the universe, its immensity and mystery; the girl thinks, 'I must wash my hair.' When I read this I was frantically upset; I had to put the magazine down. It was clear to me at once that I was not thinking as the girl thought; the full moon would never as long as I lived remind me to wash my hair. (pp. 177-78)

Dell rips up the magazine and tries to forget it.

> Afterwards [she said] when I would see an article in a magazine called 'Femininity – It's Making a Comeback' or a quiz for teenagers with a heading 'Is Your Problem that You're Trying to Be a Boy?' I would turn the page quickly as if something was trying to bite me. Yet it had never occurred to me to want to be a boy. (p. 178).

It is quite certain that Dell, like Sybylla, would also have been revolted at the 'prospect of settling down to act tame hen in a tin pot circle, and to acknowledge men superior merely owing to accident of gender' (*My Career Goes Bung*, p. 12). Miles Franklin's rebellion was not against being a female but against the role set down for females by the church and patriarchal society.

Again she was not opposed to marriage as an institution. Sybylla makes it clear that her rejection of Harold was not a rejection of marriage *per se*. 'I believe in marriage – that is, I think it the most sensible and respectable arrangement for the replenishment of a nation which has yet been suggested' (*My Brilliant Career*, p. 224). These were ideas which were echoed in *Life and Labor*. As Drusilla Modjeska points out, 'the family and marriage as institutions were never questioned but assumed to be the natural lot of most women'. However, Modjeska continues, 'although most of its fictional heroines made happy marriages *Life and Labor* pointed out that for the vast majority of women marriage meant hardship and a withdrawal "from broad social relationships"',[17] a withdrawal that Miles Franklin would reject.

One must also look at the prevailing conditions to further understand Miles Franklin's attitude. At that time sex would lead almost inevitably to pregnancy. Without contraception's freedom to choose and limit, the woman became little more than a brood sow, an incubator, a role, surprising as it may seem to Colin Roderick (R, p. 122), that Miles Franklin was unwilling to accept. The fate of these women is described by Michael Cannon in *Life in the Country*:

> Lonely grinding poverty, usually on the very edge of bankruptcy, was their common lot, with the monotonous drudgery relieved only by an occasional visit from a neighbour or travelling hawker. The amount of sheer physical labour these women had to get through each day was enormous... During harsher times, some families tried to survive without substantial protein of any

kind... Important to the farm economy was the work of tending fowls and milking cows... Such activities were universally regarded as women's work: even in 1946 ... more than half the wives on Winnera farms still milked the cows ... since the farmer could rarely afford to hire labour, he relied on breeding a large family to relieve his physical burdens. To the wife's other problems, therefore, must be added the fact that she was practically always pregnant or nursing new babies, often in filthy conditions which meant that half of them died and the effort must have been wasted to that extent.[18]

Is it any wonder that Miles Franklin railed against conditions such as these? Under them there could be no room for the career she so desperately wanted.

I believe, however, that Miles Franklin's rejection of marriage went deeper than the reasons I have already given. Above all I believe that what she was rejecting was the notion of woman as a colony to be conquered and possessed. It is commonplace today to link women's oppression with colonization, as we see, for example, in Annette Kolodny's book *The Lay of the Land*[19] and George Lamming's novel *Natives of My Person*[20] which represents one of the most explicit and detailed discussions of this relationship in post-colonial fiction.

Both the woman and the land are objects to be penetrated, conquered and possessed, victims of both capitalism and patriarchy. If the relationship is looked at in this way, one can understand man's joy in discovering that the woman is a virgin. For what conquerer/explorer can resist the pleasure of being first. After all there are not many like John Wilkes of Wilkes and Liberty fame who 'prefer expert co-operation to dewy-eyed innocence'.[21] Being first also means that no-one else has laid previous claim and thus the conqueror establishes his right to ownership.

What is more, untamed women, like untamed lands, present not only a challenge but also a threat to man's notion of his own superiority, an idea which is clearly illustrated in Shirley Hazzard's *The Transit of Venus*, a novel which makes direct links between class, gender and race. Paul

Ivory feels threatened by Caro's self-sufficiency – she is at this time a virgin. He decides that 'her self-sufficiency had given her some small degree of power over him – power that could only be reversed by an act of possession'.[22] This linking of sexual possession to power is also a dominating feature of *Natives of My Person*. As Pinteados reminds the male colonizers in that novel, 'you have had power – Everyone here has had power. To have had a woman is to know some power some time.'[23] Compare this with his later statement about the male colonizers:

> To be within the orbit of power! There they were at home. But they had to avoid the touch of power itself. The women are absolute evidence of what I mean. To feel authority over the women! That was enough for them. But to commit themselves fully to what they felt authority over. That they could never master. Such power they were afraid of.[24]

Such ideas were not in vogue in Miles Franklin's time and Miles Franklin herself was not to make the links between class, gender and racial oppression that are made today. However, I would contend that consciously or not she did perceive sex with men as the archetypal moment of male supremacy and would agree with the Leeds Revolutionary Feminists (though she wouldn't like them) that 'only in the system that is male supremacy does the oppressor actually invade and abuse the interior of the oppressed'[25] with all that this connotes in terms of possession, ownership, and power.

In support of my thesis I would refer you to Harold's attitude and Sybylla's response:

H. 'Well I can *have* you now.' (*My Brilliant Career*, p. 222)
H. 'Now that I know you care for me, I will *have* you.' (*My Brilliant Career*, p. 223)
S. 'The calm air of *ownership* with which Harold drew near annoyed me.' (*My Brilliant Career*, p. 125)
H. 'I'll be along in a week or two to *take possession* of you' (*My Brilliant Career*, p. 208)
(My emphasis.)

Harold agrees that the marriage need not be immediate: 'There's plenty of time. I don't want to hurry you, only I want you to be engaged to me *for safety*' (*My Brilliant Career*, p. 144; my emphasis). The ring he offers Sybylla serves as a down payment, so to speak, to secure possession and to indicate ownership. The ring as a symbol of colonization and enslavement is a common enough image. One has only to think of *Heart of Darkness*. The manacles round the Africans are obvious signs of their enslavement. Not perhaps so obvious but just as real a sign of colonization, is the white celluloid collar around the neck of the accountant which symbolizes not only his total commitment to, but at the same time his enslavement by, notions of white supremacy and domination. Colonizer and colonized alike are trapped within the vicious circle. On a sexual level we see the same dual aspect of enslavement in operation in *Natives of My Person*. I am referring to the wedding ring that Steward wears on a chain around his neck. The ring has been returned to him by his wife but his insistence on wearing it symbolizes his refusal to relinquish power over her and at the same time indicates that such a refusal means that the ring hangs around his neck much as the albatross did around the neck of the Ancient Mariner. The ring, we are told, 'was like a knot of feathers ... It had become a prison around his flesh'.[26] In the light of the above it is easy to see why Sybylla refused to let Harold place the ring on her finger.

Colin Roderick makes much of what he sees as the confused state of mind both of Miles Franklin and her heroines, i.e., the seeming contradiction between their flirtatious attitude and their rejection of marriage. If they were so repelled by marriage, he asks, then why flirt in the first place? There seems to me to be a perfectly obvious answer to that question. The woman (young girl) is torn between her desire for freedom, her rejection of possession, a life of her own in which she can pursue her career, and her desire to conform, to be like everyone else. 'All women,'

Shirley Hazzard writes, 'evidently longed to marry, and on leaving school held their breath, while accumulating linen and silver'[27] and waiting for the ring, the ring which would remove them from the category which Christina Stead describes as 'The Great Unwanted'. The fear of belonging to that group leads the unmarried girls into that degrading act of leaping for the bridal bouquet, a leap that reveals 'their naked need'.[28]

The pressure to conform would come not only from one's group but also from one's peer group – after all, who wants an outcast as a member of the family? In addition, the girl would have been subjected to constant reinforcement of the 'norm' by the dominant culture and ideology, backed up by the songs of persuasion – 'The Girl that I Marry', 'Paper Doll', the strains of singing 'There Goes My Only Possession' and those songs that spelt out the consequences of failure, for example, 'Silver Dollar' and the final words of its refrain:

A man without a woman is like a wreck upon the sand
There's only one thing worse in the universe
And that's a woman
Without a Man.

Women today are still faced with the choice of a career or marriage and a family, a dilemma which is discussed by numerous female writers including Margaret Atwood and Barbara Hanrahan. In her novel, significantly called *Kewpie Doll*, the latter takes up this issue. Her heroine feels split between two roles: 'I was two people – the one with nylon knees on the bike, arms around his waist, my chin tucked into his shoulder';[29] the other one wanted a career as an artist. The pressure to conform suddenly becomes so great that she decides to abandon her ambitions and to become 'the Saturday night girl, adorably feminine... I didn't want that part of myself that kept looking forward to pushing myself away from them all, to starting on that journey to aloneness' (pp. 143-44).

I would suggest that the strongest of women, and I include Miles Franklin in this category, must have at some time or other a desire to be a 'Saturday night girl'. In retrospect Miles Franklin might look back as she does in *All That Swagger* and declare that 'once curiosity has been satisfied, monotony sets in',[30] a remark Colin Roderick would no doubt attribute to sour grapes, but it seems to me that it needs a great deal of strength when one is young to resist the emotional rape of romantic love, the engagement ring and the walk down the aisle in white as the organ booms out the Wedding March. Miles Franklin did resist it, and at a time when the feminist ideas and support groups that flourish today were not in existence, but I believe she paid a high price for it.

If I may look briefly at the cost of Miles Franklin's decision. Sex outside of marriage like 'living in sin' or at Paddington (a 'Bohemian' Sydney suburb) was not fashionable then, and for anyone as prudish as Miles Franklin was not to be contemplated. 'Only in marriage can respectable women satisfy curiosity' (*My Brilliant Career*, p. 229). For her the choice of a career as an artist rather than marriage automatically meant celibacy. I mention the question of celibacy in particular because part of the stigma of being an old maid was in 'dying wondering'. It's all very well for Germaine Greer to head an article 'Better no sex than bad sex'. We accept it because she's had it. We know because she's told us. But what if one hasn't had it? One of the most vivid descriptions of how society regarded such women is to be found in Christina Stead's *For Love Alone*. Teresa, Stead's heroine, is sitting on a ferry in Sydney.

> Thinking about married women and old maids. Even the frowsiest, most ridiculous old maid on the boat, trying to shoulder her way into the inner circle of scandalmongers, getting in her drop of poison, just to show that she knew what was what, was yet more innocent looking than even a young married woman. They, of course, hushed their voices when such a person butted her way in. She might talk coarsely and laugh at smut but they saw

to it that she missed the choicest things; and of course, when they talked about childbed and breastfeeding, she had to sit with downcast eyes, ashamed. As for the secret lore that they passed round, about their husbands, she could never know that. The unmarried were foolish, round-eyed, even in old age with a round-cheeked look (or was that just her Aunt Di?) and even when withered, with pursed lips as if about to swallow a large juicy tropical fruit. That was the way they looked when they talked about the sexes! Poor wretches! ... Say what you would, she was just a battling old maid and did not know what man was like, whether Mr Wrong or Mr Right.[31]

For one who feared ridicule and pity as much as Miles Franklin this must have been a hard role to play. That she knew what society thought can be seen by her description of Della in *All That Swagger*. 'It looked as if Della might be an old maid – a failure and a disgrace.'[32] There can be no doubt that she would be bitter about such an attitude just as she would have been about the reader's report from the American publisher's on *The Net of Circumstances*. 'The book,' he said, 'placed too much stress on advanced feminist views.' The heroine is dismissed as a 'discontented old maid'.[33] The novel deals with the penalties a woman pays if she chooses a career rather than marriage and in particular with the question of motherhood.

Miles Franklin believed in race regeneration and who could make better mothers than the intelligent, liberated women (she would include herself in that category). Yet by choosing to remain unmarried she excluded herself from the role of motherhood. Intellectually, she could argue for her right to be like Father O'Toole, a spiritual parent to her country with her books as her children, but emotionally this must have been a hard decision to take. A number of her novels explore this cost, in particular *The Net of Circumstances*. That it was her own situation is fairly obvious and this accounts for her use of a pseudonym. Jill Roe tells us that when Miles Franklin in 1920 was searching for a publisher for 'Love Letters of a Superfluous Woman' she wrote, 'there is too much real feeling in these observations for me to be easy in attaching my name'.' The same would apply to *The Net of Circumstances*. The fact that this novel was published in 1915 and yet has only recently been established as being by Miles Franklin shows just how careful she was to cover her tracks. This secrecy was no doubt due partly to fear of exposing her own raw feeling but also because of the failure of her authorship. If one takes into account that so many of these brain children of hers were stillborn or died in infancy (the royalty statement for *The Net of Circumstances* records no sales),[35] then the penalty she paid for her choice to remain single was a high one indeed, and it is not surprising that Miles Franklin was both despairing and bitter.

Cassandra Pybus has suggested that Miles Franklin was attempting to create an alternate kind of love story which reflected her own ideal of spiritual unity and platonic love and I believe this is true. There are contradictions in her life and in the novels in which she struggled to resolve these contradictions. Her fiction shows her groping for a medium in which to express certain ideas and being unable to find it. She was aware of what she was trying to do and claimed her right to do so. In her work of criticism, *Laughter Not for a Cage*, she remarked that for decades male novelists had been talking of pure angelic love and restricting it to females, '...couldn't the women writers out of logical wish-fulfillment, conjure up Sir Galahads to make matched pairs'.[36]

Colin Roderick would no doubt subscribe to T. Inglis Moore's theory that there was nothing homosexual about mateship/male friendship[37] – as long as it remained within the world of the male Anglo Saxon/Celt. But once it moved outside that world it assumed a different hue. For example, Roderick tells us that Miles Franklin railed 'vociferously against the natural sexual order' and would 'yell for platonic relationships between women. If men could be mates why not women?' (R, p. 64). 'She repeatedly wanted to know *and that with overstated passion* [my emphasis] why wo women could not be pals without being considered esbians' (R, p. 72). As the authors of *Women and Society: An Australian Study* point out: 'Mateship, it has become lear ... does not apply to Aborigines, to non-European mmigrants, or to women.'[38]

If the men Miles Franklin lets her heroines marry when he permits them to marry at all seem unsuitable, think of hat other cygnet who also chose a remarkable marriage partner. I am of course referring to Dorothea in *Middlemarch*, who is appalled at the idea of marriage to Sir James Chettham and chooses Mr Casaubon instead. We are not at all surprised that there are no off-spring from that partnership, indeed I am sure we would have been amazed if here had been.

Miles Franklin was not the first to seek a spiritual relationship, a marriage of true minds. The authors of *The Mad Woman in the Attic* have argued that the essential relationship that Charlotte Brontë was seeking in *Jane Eyre* was a spiritual one, and it is quite possible that they are correct. Look at Brontë's revenge on Rochester for his attempted seduction, and see what she reduces him to before she will allow her heroine to marry him. Again in Shirley Hazzard's novel, *The Transit of Venus*, we accept the intensity of the love relationship between Caro and Ted Tice, but it s never physically consummated. In Miles Franklin's own time we have the example of Olive Schreiner. She, like Miles Franklin, believed that 'the endeavour of woman to adjust herself to the new conditions of life' would lead not towards a greater sexual laxity, or promiscuity', but to a closer, more permanent, more emotionally and intellectually complete and intimate relation between the individual man and woman', to an understanding 'that noble as is the function of the physical reproduction of humanity by the union of man and woman, rightly viewed, that union has in it latent, other, and even higher forms of creative energy and life-dispensing power, and that its history on earth has only begun'.[39]

It is such a union that I believe Miles Franklin was seeking. See, for instance, her description of the man she would marry. It would be 'one who could put his finger on some hidden spring in himself and in me and in grand fusion reveal the fullness of life' (*My Career Goes Bung* p. 228). If we are to believe what she writes in her Notebook, she finally despaired of finding such a person: 'Oneness in marriage: it is impossible. After the first flush of passion has subsided each regains separateness.'[40]

The themes of psychic loneliness and despair dominate many of her books just as they dominated her life. That doesn't seem strange to me. Neither does it seem strange that she was at times confused – most pioneers of any movement must have moments of doubt when they question both themselves and the causes for which they are struggling. Miles Franklin, I believe, was a remarkable woman, not only because she had the opinions which she had but even more so because she was brave enough to voice them when she did, and set them within the contemporary realist context. Here she joins company with William Lane whom Michael Wilding points out was 'in advance of most of his contemporaries in his awareness and stress on the women's issue'.[41] Lane, unlike Miles Franklin whose so-called egalitarianism never extended to socialism, was a socialist who saw a direct link between the class and feminist issues, a link which he explored in *The Workingman's Paradise* which was published in 1892. I make the point about the contemporary realist setting because there were several writers at that time who were also interested in 'the women's issue' but resorted to science fiction to discuss it, possibly because they felt that any solution was still light years away. Notable amongst them was Sir Julius Vogel who in his novel *Anno Domini 2000 or Women's Destiny* (1889) explored the thesis that 'a recognized dominance of either sex is unnecessary' and Mary Ann Moore-Bentley (Mrs E.H. Ling). The latter not only felt the necessity to move to another century to discuss her thesis but as the title of her novel *A Woman of Mars or, Australia's Enfranchised Woman* (1901) indicates, she also found it necessary to move to another planet. Miles Franklin was far too honest and rebellious to resort to such subterfuges.

To compare and contrast the book and the film I have discussed and to say which was closer to reality was not such a difficult task. A much harder one was to say just what the reality was. Miles Franklin is no easy subject as the titles of essays on her indicate: Marjorie Barnard, 'Who Was Miles Franklin and What Was She?'; Beatrice Davis, 'An Enigmatic Woman'; Cassandra Pybus, 'The Real Miles Franklin?'; Jill Roe, 'The Significant Silence: Miles Franklin's Middle Years'. 'She is a curious character,' Drusilla Modjeska writes, 'hard to pin down, contradictory and idiosyncratic'; and Marjorie Barnard, her friend and biographer, remarked: 'Who knows exactly what Miles felt – even when she told you?' My picture of Miles Franklin is of a sad, lonely and finally bitter person, a bitterness I believe to be caused by a feeling of a lack of achievement and fulfillment. One senses that she felt she had sacrificed so much for an ambition, a dream, and that in the end she believed it had all been in vain. I would hope that she found the consolation that Olive Schreiner spoke of in the epigraph to this paper. My fear is that she didn't.

At sixteen Miles/Sybylla had gained an insight into women's situation which few women of her time, and many women even today, never achieve. Her tragedy was that she was a woman who lived out of her time. Like that other cygnet, she was 'the off-spring of a certain spiritual grandeur ill-matched with the meanness of opportunity and with the times'.[42] Colin Roderick's attitude to her life and what she achieved is summed up in his remark: 'They [her ideas] were to issue in the sudden youthful outpouring that she called *My Brilliant Career*, insisting on the tautological question mark that everyone else struck out' (R, p. 59). I would like to refer Colin Roderick and other denigrators of Miles Franklin to the Finale of the manuscript and of the first published version of *Middlemarch*, a work with which I believe *My Brilliant Career* has many things in common. It reads:

> Certainly those determining acts of her life were not totally beautiful. They were the mixed result of young and noble impulse struggling against prosaic conditions... While this is the social air in which mortals begin to breathe, there will be collisions such as those in Dorothea's life, where great feelings will take the aspect of error, and great faith the aspect of illusion.

As Jill Roe has remarked, Miles Franklin's silent struggle to become a writer may not seem to be part of the 'Australian Dream', but then it depends on whose dreams you are talking about.[43]

NOTES

* In the language of the Australian bush the one who takes the outside track travels alone.

1. Elaine Showalter, *A Literature of Their Own: British Women Novelists from Brontë to Lessing* (London: Virago, 1978).
2. Frances McInherny, 'Miles Franklin, *My Brilliant Career* and the Female Tradition', *Australian Literary Studies*, Vol. 9, No. 3, 1980, 275-285.
3. Delys Bird, 'Towards an Aesthetics of Australian Women's Fiction: *My Brilliant Career* and *The Getting of Wisdom*', *Australian Literary Studies*, Vol. 11, No. 2, 1983, 171-181.
4. Cassandra Pybus, 'The Real Miles Franklin?', *Meanjin*, Vol. 42, No. 2, 1983, 459.
5. *My Brilliant Career* (Virago, 1980). All further references are to this edition and are included in the text.
6. Patrick White, 'Clay', in *The Burnt Ones* (London: Eyre & Spottiswoode, 1964), p. 116.
7. Colin Roderick, *Miles Franklin: Her Brilliant Career* (Sydney: Rigby, 1982). All further references are to this edition and are included in the text.

8. Shirley Hazzard, Statement in *Australian Literary Studies*, Vol. 10, No. 2, 1981, 207.

9. Virginia Woolf, *A Room of One's Own* (London: Granada, 1983), p. 6.

10. Miles Franklin, *My Career Goes Bung* (London: Virago, 1981). All further references are to this edition and are included in the text.

11. Brent of Bin Bin, *Prelude to Waking* (Sydney: Angus & Robertson, 1950). Author's note p. vii. See also Sybylla's remark in *My Career Goes Bung*: 'The book was a companion as well as an entertainment, a confidant and a twin soul' (p. 38).

12. See, for example, Chapter Seven of Christina Stead's *For Love Alone* (London: Virago, 1978).

13. George Eliot, *Middlemarch* (Harmondsworth: Penguin), pp. 424-25.

14. As a matter of fact, Roderick is reiterating patriarchal attitudes from last century. Compare Thackeray's comments about Charlotte Brontë:

> The poor little woman of genius! The fiery little eager brave tremulous homely-faced creature! I can read a great deal of her life as I fancy her in her book [*Villette*] and see that rather than have fame, rather than any other earthly good or mayhap heavenly one, she wants some Tomkins or another to love her and be in love with. But you see she is a little bit of a creature without a pennyworth of good looks, thirty years old I should think, buried in the country, and eating up her own heart there and no Tomkins will come. You girls with pretty faces will get dozens of young fellows fluttering about you – whereas here is one genius, a noble heart longing to mate itself and destined to wither away into old maidenhood with no chance to fulfil the burning desire.

And her publisher John Smith:

> There was but little feminine charm about her, and of this fact she was herself uneasily and perpetually conscious... I believe she would have given all her genius and all her fame to have been beautiful.

15. One is here reminded of Lydgate in *Middlemarch*. In spite of the fact that Rosamond had thwarted and frustrated him in every way, and in many ways was responsible for his downfall, he was still unable to think of her as an equal. 'It was inevitable,' we are told, that 'he should think of her as if she were an animal of another and feebler species.' But, as the next sentence reminds us, 'Nevertheless she had mastered him.' How dearly Lydgate paid for his belief that Rosamond was a lesser creature. (George Eliot, *Middlemarch*, p. 719.)

16. Alice Munro, *Lives of Girls and Women* (Harmondsworth: Penguin, 1986), p. 177. All further references are to this edition and are included in the text.

17. Drusilla Modjeska, *Exiles at Home* (Sydney: Angus & Robertson, 1981), p. 164.

18. Michael Cannon, *Life in the Country*, quoted by Susan Gardiner in her commentary to *My Brilliant Career*, South African edition (Johannesburg: David Phillip, 1982), p. 258.

19. Annette Kolodny, *The Lay of the Land* (Chapel Hill: University of North Carolina Press, 1975).

20. George Lamming, *Natives of My Person* (London: Longman, 1972).

21. Quoted by C.C. Trench, *Portrait of a Patriot: A Biography of John Wilkes* (Edinburgh & London: William Blackwood, 1962).

22. Shirley Hazzard, *The Transit of Venus* (Harmondsworth: Penguin, 1981), p. 98.

23. *Natives of My Person*, p. 180.

24. *Natives of My Person*, p. 325.

25. Quoted by Elizabeth Wilson in her essay 'I'll Climb the Stairway to Heaven: Lesbianism in the Seventies', in *Sex and Love*, eds. Sue Cartledge and Joanna Ryan (London: The Women's Press, 1983), p. 188.

26. *Natives of My Person*, pp. 200 and 190.

27. Shirley Hazzard, *The Transit of Venus*, p. 48.

28. Christina Stead, *For Love Alone*, p. 39.

29. Barbara Hanrahan, *Kewpie Doll* (London: Chatto & Windus, 1984), p. 109. All further references are to this edition and are included in the text.

30. Miles Franklin, *All That Swagger* (Sydney: Angus & Robertson, 1974), p. 418.

31. Christina Stead, *For Love Alone*, pp. 16-17 and p. 38.

32. Miles Franklin, *All That Swagger*, p. 217.

33. Quoted by Jill Roe in 'The Significant Silence: Miles Franklin's Middle Years', *Meanjin*, 1980, No. 1, 56.

34. Jill Roe, p. 57.

35. Jill Roe, p. 57.

36. Miles Franklin, *Laughter Not for a Cage* (Sydney: Angus & Robertson, 1974). Quoted by Ray Matthew in *Miles Franklin* (Melbourne: Oxford University Press, 1963), p. 19.

37. T. Inglis Moore, *Social Patterns in Australian Literature* (Sydney: Angus & Robertson, 1971), p. 224; see Chapter IX, 'The Creed of Mateship'. Inglis Moore was to dismiss Richard Mahony, Stan Parker and Voss as un-Australian because none of them possessed a mate!

38. Sol Encel, Norman MacKenzie and Margaret Tebbits, *Women and Society: An Australian Study* (Melbourne: Cheshire, 1974), p. 42.
39. Olive Schreiner, *Woman and Labour* (London: Virago, 1978), pp. 25-26.
40. Miles Franklin, Notebook, p. 88 (Mitchell Library, MS 1360).
41. Michael Wilding in Introduction to *The Workingman's Paradise* (Sydney: Sydney University Press, 1980), p. 51.
42. George Eliot, *Middlemarch*, p. 25.
43. Jill Roe, pp. 57-58.

The Getting of Wisdom: Individuality vs. Conformity

JENNIFER BREEN

Henry Handel Richardson's semi-autobiographical novel, *The Getting of Wisdom* (1910), despite its superficially unpromising setting of a Presbyterian ladies' college in Melbourne during the 1880s, attracts male as well as female readers internationally. Virago reissued this work in 1981 as one of their 'Modern Classics'; *The Times Educational Supplement* reprinted a central chapter from this work on 21 August 1981; and the Rabelaisian *Unreliable Memoirs* (1980) of the cosmopolitan Clive James are prefaced with an epigraph acknowledging 'the getting of wisdom'. Thus this novel seems to have a universal as well as a feminist appeal: but what is the secret of this dual attraction?

Let us consider, firstly, its universal themes. The main setting of this novel – the boarding-school which the heroine, Laura, attends with fifty-five other girls from the age of twelve to the age of sixteen – is a microcosm of Australian bourgeois society towards the end of the nineteenth century.[1] Some of the main obsessions of the girls at the school, as in their wider social milieu, are income or the lack of it, a profession (for men) or the lack of it, and the consciousness of being 'colonials'.

When Laura first arrives at the school, her fellow pupils are agog to know the following:

> 'What's your father?'
> 'He's dead,' answered the child.
> 'Well, but I suppose he was alive once wasn't he, duffer? What was he before he was dead?'
> 'A barrister.'
> 'What did he die of?'
> 'Consumption.'
> 'How many servants do you keep?'
> 'One.'
> 'How much have you got a year?'
> 'I don't know.'[2]

And so on. Laura is actually poor, and her mother does embroidery for a living, a fact which Laura, apart from one instance of impulsive confiding which she regrets, tries to conceal from everyone. Above all, Laura, like the other girls, is aware that

> loud as money made itself in this young community, effectual as it was in cloaking shortcomings, it did not go all the way: inherited instincts and traditions were not so easily subdued. Just some of the wealthiest too, were aware that their antecedents would not stand a close scrutiny.... Yet Laura knew very well that good birth and an aristocratic appearance would not avail her, did the damaging fact leak out that Mother worked for her living. (pp. 95-96)

Laura's sympathies at the age of twelve or thirteen are more wideranging than those of her classmates, however, which enables her to understand a poverty-stricken girl who steals from those who are well-off:

> she had understood Annie Johns' motive better than anyone else. Well, she had no business to understand – that was the long and the short of it: nice-minded girls found such a thing impossible, and turned incuriously away... Oh! the last wish in the world she had was to range herself on the side of the sinner; she longed to see eye to eye with her comrades – if she had only known how to do it... And the child's feelings, as she stood at

the window, were not very far removed from prayer. Had they found words, they would have taken the form of an entreaty that she might be preserved from having thoughts that were different from other people's; that she might be made to feel as she ought to feel, in a proper, ladylike way – and especially did she see a companion convicted of crime. (pp. 107-108)

But, of course, what Laura hopes to be 'preserved from' – 'having thoughts that were different from other people's' – is what the reader admires: her ability to stand apart and observe accurately the effects of a class system that is based on money.

The following episode, however, brings out another subtle pressure – besides that of social class – at the school: the necessity for each girl to make her social behaviour conform to the general mould in order to have desirable friends. Although one of her fellow schoolgirls, Chinky, has a 'crush' on her, Laura realizes that friendship with her would not make her any more popular. Chinky is a boarder from a family with little money whom, sadly, no one likes. In her relationship with Chinky, Laura shows little or no understanding:

> Chinky had been dismissed – privately because she was a boarder – from the school. Her crime was: she had taken half-a-sovereign from the purse of one of her room-mates. When taxed with the theft, she wept that she had not taken it for herself, but to buy a ring for Laura Rambotham; and, with this admission on her lips, she passed out of their lives...
>
> Laura had not cared two straws for Chinky; she found what the latter had done, 'mean and disgusting', and said so, stormily; but of course was not believed. (p. 163)

Here Laura is trying to dissociate herself from the culprit, Chinky, partly because she had inadvertently encouraged Chinky to buy her a ring, and partly because she had already been found out as a person who tells lies, and now does not wish to be completely cast out of school society because the girls think she has helped someone to steal.

146

This universal fear of being cast out – whether by force or by choice – from 'civilized' society is another dominant theme in *The Getting of Wisdom*. This fear was possibly exacerbated in Australia of the 1880s because the seeds of the early colony lay in Britain's casting out of some of her wrongdoers to the other side of the world. But two kinds of expulsion exist at Laura's school: being thrust out of the school for some major offence such as stealing, and being ostracized by other pupils within the school because of a lack of conformity to minor social rules.

And Laura was a constant infringer of these unwritten rules. A humorous example of this propensity is in Laura's visit to the drawing-room of the English-born school Principal and his wife, Mr and Mrs Strachey, where she dismisses classical music in favour of pieces such as 'Home, Sweet Home', and is over-familiar with the Principal. The Lady Superintendent – that is, the Headmistress – Mrs Gurley, punishes her:

> Mrs Gurley had crushed and humiliated her. Laura learnt that she had been guilty of a gross impertinence, in profaning the ears of the Principal and Mrs Strachey with Thalberg's music, and that all the pieces she had brought with her from home would now be taken from her. Secondly, Mr Strachey had been so unpleasantly impressed by the boldness of her behaviour, that she would not be invited to the drawing-room again for some time to come.
>
> The matter of the music touched Laura little: if they preferred their dull old exercises to what she had offered them, so much the worse for them. But the reproach cast on her manners stung her even more deeply than it had done when she was still the raw little newcomer: for she had been pluming herself of late that she was now 'quite the thing'. (p. 82)

Here lies the pattern of Laura's behaviour: she does her utmost to fit into the school mould, but, through some spontaneous or imaginative piece of behaviour, she is constantly being cast out again. After she has been sent to Coventry for making up stories about her love affair with a curate, and for supposedly encouraging Chinky to steal in order to buy her a ring, she seems to have finally learnt to weight her words before uttering them, instead of blurting out her thoughts in the childish fashion that had exposed her to ridicule; she learnt, too, at last, to keep her real opinions to herself, and to make those she expressed tally with her hearers'. And she was quick to discover that this was a short-cut towards regaining her lost place: to conceal what she truly felt – particularly if her feelings ran counter to those of the majority. For, the longer she was at school, the more insistently the truth was driven home to her, that the majority is always in the right. (p. 178)

But Laura never does learn to subdue her feelings so that she is completely acceptable to other girls: she has a lesbian crush on an older pupil of eighteen, Evelyn, which other pupils mock, especially when Laura's behaviour becomes extreme just prior to Evelyn's departure: 'did they meet her [Laura] privately on the stairs or in a house-corridor, they crossed their hands on their breasts and turned up their eyes, tragedy-fashion' (p. 210). After Evelyn has left the school, Laura takes to religion – like many other schoolgirls have done – in order to believe that she has spiritual help in passing her final examinations. But when her prayers seem to lead her to cheating in one of these examinations in order to pass it, she is disillusioned with God: 'the more inclined she grew to think that it had been a kind of snare on the part of God, to trap her afresh into sin, and thus to prolong her dependence on him...' (p. 223). Fortunately for Laura's standing in the school, her cheating was not discovered.

Laura, despite learning 'facts' to satisfy her teachers, and acquiring the social etiquette that endears her to her schoolfellows, never succeeds in feeling that she is part of the school:

She went out from school with the uncomfortable sense of being a square peg, which fitted into none of the round holes of her world; the wisdom she had got, the experience she was richer by, had, in the process of equipping her for life, merely seemed to disclose her unfitness. She could not then know that, even for the squarest peg, the right hole may ultimately be found; seeming unfitness prove to be only another aspect of a peculiar and special fitness ... many a day came and went before she grasped that, oftentimes, just those mortals who feel cramped and unsure in the conduct of everyday life, will find themselves to rights, with astounding ease, in that freer, more spacious world where no practical considerations hamper, and where the creatures that inhabit dance to their tune: the world where are stored up men's best thoughts, the hopes, and fancies; where the shadow is the substance, and the multitude of business pales before the dream. (p. 230)

Here Richardson seems to be showing that imaginative people, in this instance, presumably authors in whose imaginary 'world ... the creatures that inhabit dance to their tune' – surmount the feeling of being 'cramped and unsure in the conduct of everyday life'. It seems to me that it is this quality in Richardson's work – that of portraying an individual that overcomes the pettiness of social constraints and develops her unique gifts – that appeals to readers. Through Laura's experience we realize that it is possible to preserve our individuality and uniqueness without being cast out from society.

The conclusion of this novel, in which Laura runs freely away from the school, symbolizes the fact that the school has not tamed her:

'I'm going to have a good run,' said Laura; and tightened her hair-ribbon.
'Oh, but you can't run in the street! You're too big. People'll see you.'
'Think I care? – If you'd been years only doing what you were allowed to, I guess you'd want to do something you weren't allowed to, too. – Good-bye!' (p. 232)

Laura's running demonstrates how no totalitarian society – and Laura's school is totalitarian in that Mrs Gurley rules it 'through fear' (p. 55) – can channel or suppress the thoughts and feelings of all its members. Men enjoy this novel presumably because freedom, or the lack of it, is a problem not only for feminists, but for everyone.

149

Now, secondly, let us examine the feminist aspects of this novel, which is one of several early to mid-twentieth-century works by Australian women writers who emphasize the need for individuals of both sexes to pursue a classless social freedom, but especially for women, who, in a still relatively formless culture and society, could grasp opportunities for developing their own independent selves. Richardson shows that she is aware of the kind of money-based class system that developed in Australia, and in her portrayal of Laura she demonstrates how typing people by class membership is constricting and repressive. Moreover, Richardson is also aware that, to be able to develop freely, her heroine must overturn her socio-economic class membership *and* sexual gender: 'seeming unfitness' must be shown 'to be only another aspect of a peculiar and special fitness' (p. 230).

So, writing in 1910, what does Richardson have to tell us about the effects of belonging to the female sex?

Firstly, girls are brought up to think that a deep interest in the 'personal', rather than in the factual and scientific, is naturally feminine. Different kinds of girls co-exist at the Presbyterian ladies' college, from the few who are interested in knowledge to the majority who are unambitiously sunk in becoming well-servanted Hausfraus. Thus one of the visiting teachers, Miss Hicks, castigates one of her pupils:

> 'I'll tell you what it is, Inez,' she said, 'you're blessed with a real woman's brain: vague, slippery, inexact, interested only in the personal aspect of a thing. You can't concentrate your thoughts, and, worst of all, you've no curiosity – about anything that really matters. You take all the great facts of existence on trust – just as a hen does – and I've no doubt you'll go on contentedly till the end of your days, without ever knowing why the ocean has tides, and what causes the seasons. – It makes me ashamed to belong to the same sex.' (p. 75)

Note how Miss Hicks adopts the fallacy, still common, that women's brains are fundamentally different from men's.

Nevertheless, she also seems to believe that women can develop the so-called 'masculine' qualities of thought, and by that she means the rigorously logical and scientific. Richardson, in her comment in her author's voice that the class 'tittered furiously, let the sarcasm glide over them unlit by its truth' (p. 75), shows that she shares Miss Hicks' views. Laura 'felt humiliated... She did not want to have a woman's brain' and thus she set out to suppress her intuitive and imaginative knowledge in favour of the

> facts that were wanted of her; facts that were the real test of learning; facts she was expected to know. Stories, pictures of things, would not help her an inch along the road. Thus, it was not the least use in the world to her to have seen the snowy top of Mount Kosciusko stand out against a dark blue evening sky, and to know its shape to a tittlekin. On the other hand, it mattered tremendously that this mountain was 7308 and not 7309 feet high: that piece of information was valuable, was of genuine use to you; for it was worth your place in the class. (p. 77)

Elsewhere in the novel Richardson portrays a character who supposedly thinks in a 'masculine' way: Mary Pidwall, known to all as M. Pidwall, or M.P., has 'a kind of manly exactness in her habit of thinking and speaking; and it was this trait her companions tried to symbolize, in calling her by the initial letters of her name' (p. 154). But M. Pidwall's ambition to get a degree at Trinity College and to run her own school is destined to fail: 'Within six months of leaving school, M.P. married and settled down in her native township; and thereafter she was forced to adjust the rate of her progress to the steps of halting little feet' (p. 229). In fact, the majority of the girls at the school are bound for only the one career – if it can be called that – of childbearing, hostessing, and servant-bossing.

Nevertheless a few of Laura's friends had ambitions similar to those of ambitious men. The members of the school Literary Society, formed by about twenty girls, wrote their stories and essays under their surnames only. When Laura is admitted she is invited as '"a new author,

Rambotham, who it is hoped will prove a valuable acquisition to the Society, to read us his maiden effort"' (p. 189). Perhaps the source of Richardson's decision to write under a male pseudonym goes back to her own schooldays, because she not only then associated manliness with both exactness of mind and independence of spirit, but also with this joke of parodying manliness.

But in portraying her heroine's sexual ambivalence Richardson changes her style from comic realism to melodrama. Laura's first encounters with heterosexuality are treated humorously with an edge of realism; for example, we learn that the only source of sexual knowledge that the girls have access to is the Bible, and consequently their knowledge of sexuality is mostly fantasy:

> rhymes circulated that would have staggered a back-blocker; while the governesses were without exception, young and old, kindly and unkindly, laid under such flamboyant suspicions as the poor ladies had, for certain, never heard breathed – since their own impudent schooldays.
>
> This dabbling in the illicit – it had little in common with the opener grime of the ordinary schoolboy – did not even widen the outlook of these girls. For it was something to hush up and keep hidden away...
>
> For out of it all rose the vague, crude picture of woman as the prey of man. Man was animal, a composite of lust and cruelty, with no aim but that of brutally taking his pleasure: something monstrous, yet to be adored; annihilating, yet to be sought after; something to flee and, at the same time, to entice, with every art at one's disposal. (p. 112)

This exaggerated partial truth is, of course, comic, as well as serious in its revelation of the ill-effects of incomplete knowledge.

Moreover, Richardson shows us the effects of this distorted knowledge on the girls' behaviour with their male friends. Laura attracts the interest of a handsome adolescent, Bob, but unfortunately for her self-image and prestige in the school, she has not mastered any of the tricks that her friends might use in captivating him. Laura learns, after she has bored her potential admirer, how she might manage the male sex:

> 'Just let him hang round, and throw sheep's-eyes, till he's as soft as a jellyfish, and when he's right down ripe, roaring mad, go off and pretend to do a mash with someone else. That's the way to glue him, chicken.' ...
> 'But you never get to know him!'
> 'Oh, hang it, Laura, but you *are* rich! What d'you think one has a boy for, I'd like to know... If you go about too much with one, you soon have to fake an interest in his rotten old affairs. Or else just hold your tongue and let him blow. And that's dull work.' (pp. 127-128)

Nothing much has changed in male-female relations in the last ninety to a hundred years.

In order to keep up with her friends – and also, as Richardson makes clear, Laura is attracted to the opposite sex – Laura determines to love Mr Shepherd, the curate, discovering that 'By dint of pretending that it was so, she gradually worked herself up into an attack of love, which was genuine enough to make her redden when Mr Shepherd was spoken of' (pp. 135-136). But, in contrast with the prosaic conventionality of her visit to the Shepherds' home, she makes up a hot-blooded account of the curate's passionate behaviour to her. Her fantasies are partly a response to the demands of her friends for 'romance', but, when Laura is found out by the Shepherds' next guest, M. Pidwall, Laura is ostracized by the whole school.

Through a combination of this experience and her writing for the Literary Society, Laura discovers the difference between art and reality, and between fiction and fact. To tell lies convincingly, as she has done, in real life, is a moral fault: to tell convincing lies in fiction is an artistic skill:

> In your speech, your talk with others, you must be exact to the point of pedantry, and never romance or draw the long-bow; or you would be branded as an abominable liar. Whereas, as soon

as you put pen to paper, provided you kept one foot planted on probability, you might lie as hard as you liked: indeed, the more vigorously you lied, the louder would be your hearers' applause. (p. 192)

The developing novelist in Laura is one of the central themes of *The Getting of Wisdom*, although Richardson herself set out on a musical career in Europe and only changed to novel-writing when she, ironically, decided to marry, and consequently gave up studying music in Leipzig. But from this semi-autobiographical novel the reader receives the impression that Richardson's main interest all along was in fiction-writing.

Previous critics have seen Henry Handel Richardson's giving up of her musical career as the result of her realizing that she was not cut out to be a great musician. Thus Vincent Buckley, quoting Leonie Kramer's view from her essay in Geoffrey Dutton's *The Literature of Australia* (Penguin, 1964), asserts: 'one critic is inclined to guess that she turned to writing during her Leipzig days out of chagrin and disappointment at finding that she was, after all, quite without musical genius. Talent was one thing, and it was no doubt pleasant to possess it, but "genius" was what really interested her.'[3]

But critics do not have to 'guess' her motives, since she sets her complicated reasoning out in her autobiography, *Myself When Young*. The main reason she gives for relinquishing her music course in Leipzig was to become engaged to marry a young Scot, J.G. Robertson, who was then a scholar in German literature:

Here was I, who had been brought to Leipzig at what, for Mother, represented a considerable outlay: on whose behalf she put up with living abroad, which she detested, among people she didn't like and whose language she could not master. Yet all this she was willing to endure, provided she might take me back to Australia a finished pianist, there to make not only money but a name for myself. For me now to blurt out that I didn't propose to put my training to any use, but, instead, contemplated marrying an insignificant young man, would be a cruel blow to her dreams and ambitions.

She persuaded her mother, however, to let them become engaged:

> The first problem was what to do with me in the interim. Apparently it did not occur to anyone to suggest that I worked on and took my certificate, so as to be qualified to add to our resources should the need arise. But in those days wives did not work. The husband alone was expected to provide the wherewithal, and thought relatively little of if he couldn't. And it suited me. For all I could have done was to teach; and, for that, my aptitude was as small as my liking.

Henry Handel Richardson by then had also realized how much she hated performing on the concert platform, and was glad to give up this part of her musical career. On the other hand, she also thought that she had a talent for musical composition that she never explored. Nevertheless, in London while waiting to be married, she found that she enjoyed writing:

> I felt that at last I had discovered what I liked best to do. To sit alone and unobserved, behind a shut door, and play with words and ponder phrases. (What a contrast to the odious publicity of the concert-platform! How I could ever have imagined myself fitted for it I didn't know.)[4]

But was this conclusion but a rationalization of her situation?

In creating the other side of Laura's sexuality – her lesbian inclinations – Richardson fails to heed what she shows her character, Laura, having learnt; that is, in art 'provided that you kept one foot planted in probability you might lie as hard as you liked'. Richardson's recounting of Laura's obsession with Evelyn, a girl two or three years older than Laura, sounds improbable, possibly because in dealing with this subject – a lesbian crush – Richardson, instead of sticking to her mode of comic realism, has fallen into melodrama. It is not the fact of a schoolgirl's crush on a person of the same sex that is improbable; it is Richardson's treatment of this theme that makes it seem unconvincing. The following juxtaposition of a comic heterosexual scene in *The Getting of Wisdom* with a melodramatic lesbian one illustrates this difference in treatment.

Here is the inexperienced Laura trying to hook the young man, Bob, who fancies himself with girls:

> Now was the moment, felt Laura, to say something very witty, or pert, or clever; and a little pulse in her throat beat hard, as she furiously racked her brains... One after the other she considered and dismissed: the pleasant coolness of the morning, the crowded condition of the street, even the fact of the next day being Sunday – ears and cheeks on fire, meanwhile, at her own slow-wittedness. And Bob smiled. She almost hated him for that smile. It was so assured, and withal so disturbing... he waited for her to make the onslaught.
>
> But he waited in vain; and when they had walked a whole street-block in this mute fashion, it was he who broke the silence.
>
> 'Ripping girls, those Woodwards,' he said, and seemed to be remembering their charms. (pp. 118-119)

Here Richardson is satirizing the awkward thirteen-year-old and her equally inept would-be lover.

But later in the novel, when Laura has failed to attract either Bob or the curate, she responds to the friendly advances of the eighteen-year-old fellow-pupil, Evelyn, who is soon to leave the school. In the following episode, Laura is enraged because in her company Evelyn has flirted with a male friend: 'Laura sat in her thin nightgown and shivered, feeling the cold intensely after the great heat of the day. She hoped with all her heart that she would be lucky enough to get an inflammation of the lungs. Then, Evelyn would be sorry she had been so cruel to her' (p. 202). Thus Richardson, without any ironic or comic note, has her heroine trying melodramatically to make herself ill.

A subsequent description of Laura's feelings also seems unrealistic:

> She was of course reconciled, she sobbed, to Evelyn marrying some day: only plain and stupid girls were left to be old maids: but it must not happen for years and years and years to come, and when it did, it must be to someone much older than herself, someone she did not greatly care for: in short, Evelyn was to marry only to escape the odium of the single life. (p. 208)

In general, rather than treating her heroine with the detached tone that she achieves elsewhere, Richardson is indulgent, suggesting that Laura's behaviour is not comical but is justified by her 'love' for Evelyn.

Richardson seems to have been aware of her artistic problem in dealing with this autobiographical episode, because in *Myself When Young* she states:

> The one episode in the story [*The Getting of Wisdom*] I deliberately weakened was my headstrong fancy for the girl there called 'Evelyn'. To have touched this in other than lightly would have been out of keeping with the tone of the book. The real thing was neither light nor amusing. It stirred me to my depths, rousing feelings I hadn't known I possessed, and leaving behind it a heartache as cruel as my first [love for a man].[5]

Despite this assertion, Richardson seems to have 'touched ... in' this experience more than 'lightly', perhaps because she recounted the events much as they actually occurred, rather than transforming her raw emotion into her chosen artistic form.

Vincent Buckley comments on 'her creative problem' in dealing with this 'Evelyn' material: 'As it appears in the novel, the emotions of this episode are not distanced and understood, they are rather held in abeyance or subjected to a process of scrambling.' Buckley, however, implies that Richardson should have given us in the novel 'the nature and scale of the anguish which Richardson later confessed she had actually experienced'.[6] But art does not consist of factual descriptions of actual events or episodes: to turn this one episode in the novel into tragic stuff would also mar this work of comic realism. The only possible artistic solution would have been to give this material the same ironic, dispassionately humorous treatment that the other episodes received.

In earlier sections of the novel, Richardson adroitly uses minor characters to comment on and expose the follies of her major characters; for example, when Laura is leaving home for the first time, Sarah, the maid, tells her over-solicitous mother, 'I guess school'll knock all the nonsense out of her' (p. 16). Or again, when Laura is trying to turn herself into a flirt, and her would-be lover, Bob, tries to play a man of the world, his father mocks them by asking Laura: '"are you aware that this son of mine is a professed lady-killer? ... Put not your trust in Robert! He's always on with the new love before he's off with the old. You ask him whose glove he's still cherishing in the pocket next his heart' (p. 121). Here Richardson is mocking pretention and false emotion.

Thus, in dealing with the overblown affair between Laura and Evelyn, Richardson treats the pair as star-crossed lovers, except for an occasional hint at the reality behind the 'romance': 'at moments – when Laura lay sobbing face downwards on her bed, or otherwise vented her pertinacious and disruly grief – at these moments she thought she scented a dash of relief in Evelyn, at the prospect of deliverance' (p. 211).

Nevertheless, Richardson's novel is an exceptional work in the semi-autobiographical mode, and, with the obvious exception of the earlier *My Brilliant Career* (1901), few other novels of this kind by Australian women authors are comparable to it. The strength of *The Getting of Wisdom* can be seen by contrasting this work with another Virago classic, the superficially similar *Frost in May* (1933) by Antonia White, which is set in a British Roman Catholic boarding-school. White's language often expires into the prose of popular women's magazines: 'Nanda's last thread of selfontrol snapped. She burst into a storm of convulsive, almost tearless sobs that wrenched all her muscles and brought no relief. The whole world had fallen away and left her stranded in this one spot alone for ever and ever with her father and those awful words.'[7] Richardson, in writing *The Getting of Wisdom*, overcame the enslaving lichés of women's popular fiction, just as she tried in her actual life to free herself from a stereotyped female role.

NOTES

. See Leonie Kramer, *Myself When Laura: Fact and Fiction in Henry Handel Richardson's School Career* (Melbourne: Heinemann Educational Books, 1966). For a detailed account of Richardson's life and work, see Dorothy Green, *Ulysses Bound: Henry Handel Richardson and her Fiction* (Canberra: Australian National University Press, 1973).

. Henry Handel Richardson, *The Getting of Wisdom* (1910; London: Virago, 1981), p. 41. All subsequent page references for quotations from this novel are to this edition.

. Vincent Buckley, *Henry Handel Richardson*, 'Australian Writers and Their Work' Series, New Edn. (Melbourne: Oxford University Press, 1970), p. 4.

. Henry Handel Richardson, *Myself When Young* (Melbourne: Heinemann, 1948), pp. 101, 117, 126.

. *Myself When Young*, p. 70.

. *Henry Handel Richardson*, p. 25.

. Antonia White, *Frost in May* (1933; London: Virago, 1978), p. 216.

Conflicting Structures in Christina Stead's *For Love Alone*

JOHN COLMER

At the time of her death Christina Stead had won inter national recognition as a writer. But because she had neve identified herself narrowly with any one country she wa not only difficult to place but had never quite won th praise she deserved. Now that she is dead American critic claim her as a great writer on the basis of *The Man Wh Loved Children*, Australians as a great Australian writer o the basis of *For Love Alone*, and feminist critics as a grea feminist writer on the strength of both these novels, whil European critics praise her as a great European writer fo *The Salzburg Tales* and *The House of all Nations* – the latte a superb study of the Parisian banking system.

Christina Stead is one of the many Australian wome who left Australia to become a writer. Others are Mile Franklin, Henry Handel Richardson and, more recently Shirley Hazzard. In case you should think that this repre sents a complete rejection of a male-dominated society o the part of Christina Stead, it is worth recalling that i 1980 she strenuously denied that the departure of Teres Hawkins, the young Australian heroine of the novel *Fo Love Alone*, implied a rejection of Australia; rather th departure was part of the spiritual and literary odyssey necessary for any embryonic artist. Christina Stead, like her heroine Teresa, left Australia in her early twenties. Her life as a writer was spent in America, England and Europe and she only returned to Australia after the death of her husband in the late 1960s. The two novels that reflect most directly her early experience in Australia are *The Seven Poor Men of Sydney* and *For Love Alone*. In this paper I want to focus on *For Love Alone*. To begin with, I should like to show its relationship to three narrative genres and then I should like to uncover two conflicting deep structures that are never quite successfully reconciled; the one linear and optimistic and the other circular and profoundly pessimistic.

The form of *For Love Alone* is clearly related to three familiar kinds of narrative: firstly, the *Bildungsroman*, secondly the quest, and thirdly the Young Person from the Provinces novel. Like the *Bildungsroman*, it charts the formative years of a young person, who is also a potential artist. But in comparison with Joyce's *A Portrait of the Artist as a Young Man* and Lawrence's *Sons and Lovers*, the artistic potential of Stead's heroine is much more lightly sketched. Douglas Stewart complained that Teresa is a woman first and a genius second, whereas she should be a genius first and a woman second. This is to miss the whole point of the novel, which is to show that the development of Teresa's genius is dependent on her liberation as a woman. In spite of Christina Stead's angry denial in 1980 that the novel had anything to do 'with women's liberation' and her statement that 'the separation of women from men [was] the most disgraceful and disorderly thing in the movement',[1] the novel does deal with crucial issues in the feminist cause: a woman's right to dispose of her own body, the fallacy that a woman is genetically inferior to a man, the irrelevance of man-made laws to women, the fact that a woman can have honour irrespective of chastity, and her right to economic independence.

The connection of *For Love Alone* with the quest narrative is abundantly clear throughout the novel. It is announced in the Preface, expounded in a later passage that connects Teresa's voyage of discovery with the historical voyages of de Quiros and Captain Cook, and kept constantly in the reader's mind by the parallels suggested between Teresa's quest and the greatest quest narrative of all, the story of Ulysses or Odysseus. 'Each Australian is a Ulysses', we are reminded in the novel.

The third kind of novel that *For Love Alone* is related to is what Lionel Trilling once labelled *The Young Man From the Provinces*.[2] This is a tale of a young person with a limited provincial background who moves to the great metropolis and is initiated into the life of culture, art and – often – snobbery and vice. Trilling's examples are Stendhal's *Red and Black*, Flaubert's *Sentimental Education*, and James's *The Princess Casamassima*. In *For Love Alone*, Teresa Hawkins' journey from the provincial culture of Sydney in the 1930s to the metropolitan culture of London conforms to this basic model.

Many critics, taking their cue from the title, *For Love Alone*, have assumed that the novel has a single major theme, Teresa's quest for love. My own view is that this is a gross simplification and that one must also take into account other related themes, such as Teresa's quest for knowledge, her quest for freedom and equality, and her quest for independence. The pattern of the heroine's various quests can be set out in diagrammatic form. The advantage of doing so is that it immediately reveals one of the main structures of the novel. It also reveals the function of the four main men in Teresa's life in relation to that structure: her narcissistic father Andrew Hawkins, the supreme egoist Jonathan Crow, the generous melodramatic lover James Quick, and the quixotic Harry Girton. This structure is essentially linear; it marks out the main stages in the heroine's quest, one which still remains at the conclusion open-ended and unachieved. Yet it is an optimistic structure, since the development is progressive and the protagonist moves slowly closer to her goal.

Linear Structure

Solitary experience	love & knowledge	love & equality	love & independence	?
(rebellion against Andrew, family and society)	(Jonathan Crow)	(James Quick)	(Harry Girton)	

Of course, it is impossible to do justice to the complexity of the various stages and their interconnection; but at least the diagram has the merit of stressing the linear movement. It also has the other merit of noting the importance that rebellion against the father, disengagement from familial and social bonds, the quest for knowledge, sexual equality and complete independence have in Teresa's personal quest.

In contrast to this optimistic linear quest-structure, there is a very different one. This is a pessimistic circular structure. Its climax is marked by the last words of the novel when Teresa finally comes to realise how blind and deluded she had been about Jonathan Crow. 'After a while, Teresa sighed bitterly. "It's dreadful to think that it will go on being repeated for ever, he – and me! What's to stop it?"'[3] These profoundly depressing words have a rather similar effect to the last words of *Washington Square* 'for life – as it were'. They send the reader back into the novel to reconsider the real significance of the pattern of life disclosed through its deeper structures. When Teresa says 'It's dreadful to think that it will go on being repeated for ever, he – and me!', she alludes to the cycle of experience in which she and Jonathan have been imprisoned. And when she adds 'What's to stop it?', she reinforces the deterministic cycle, created by selfishness, blindness, and self-delusion. Young people will go on repeating the same

163

mistakes for ever and ever. Now this interpretation of life, as it affects Teresa and Jonathan Crow, can be represented diagrammatically as follows:

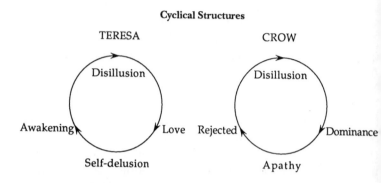

Cyclical Structures

TERESA

Disillusion

Awakening

Love

Self-delusion

CROW

Disillusion

Rejected

Dominance

Apathy

It should be obvious that the linear and cyclical structures express two contrary interpretations of life. We might say that the optimistic linear quest structure is the dominant, but that it is undercut by the pessimistic cyclic structure, which suggests that human beings are prisoners of a psychological determinism, because of idealism, blind egotism and flattering self-delusion.

Some critics have complained that Stead's style is repetitive and static. Apparently they have not seen that the repetitive and static texture reinforces the cyclical structure, since it suggests the inability of men and women to move out of a deterministic pattern; hence repetition, stasis, circularity.

So far I have noted the three genres to which *For Love Alone* is related (the *Bildungsroman*, the quest, and the Young Person from the Provinces). And I have noted that it organises its interpretation of life according to two contradictory structures – and, of course, the essence of all art is that it structures our experience into a significant pattern. Now, I should like to look at the narrative technique, the method by which the story is told.

It is an autobiographical novel – this we know from internal as well as external evidence. But it is not told in the first person as *Great Expectations* is. Yet I think Christina Stead is striving for a similar effect: to combine the immediacy of direct personal experience with a wiser, older, more objective view. If this is the case, we might ask ourselves what are some of the techniques she employs for combining subjectivity and objectivity; immediacy and detachment; immersion *in* experience and judgement *of* experience. How does Christina Stead ensure that the reader stands both inside Teresa's experience and outside it, a director participator, but yet able to evaluate it better than Teresa herself or any of the other characters?

Let me just point to a few of the techniques. First, the opening sentence of the book 'In the part of the world Teresa came from'. The ambiguity that hovers over the past tense *came* suggests that Teresa has left the upside-down world she was born in and that the narrative stance is based on the assumption that her 'buffoon odyssey' is over; that the narrator is able to see it as a whole, not as a series of random episodes as they occur in life, and as to some extent they may be imagined as occurring in Teresa's life.

Second, there is judgement of Teresa in the course of the story. This arises from a variety of techniques: (i) dramatic encounters with others in which her excesses of passion, romantic idealisation, incapacity to sympathise with others or tolerate their faults is revealed (the marvellous farewell to Crow scene in which she rejects the young man in the raincoat who is an alternative image of her own craving for affection); and (ii) techniques of ironic deflation in which Teresa's ideals and values are suddenly seen to be unreal, pretentious, overblown, and therefore in need of pricking. This is a device for pricking the balloon of her self-esteem. For instance there is much truth but not the complete truth in Crow's accusation that she is a masochist who courts sorrows and is a perfect example of mythomania (p. 442). But Teresa knows how to use the deflationary technique herself. When her vain, loquacious father foolishly repeats his absurd old-world gallantries he has spoken to the Harkness girls (he refers to them as the three graces) and when he then repeats Mina Harkness's compliment 'Oh Mr Hawkins, how very nice', Teresa promptly deflates his amorous self-esteem with the single remark: 'Do you mean that fat one?' (p. 8). In similar fashion, her father, her brothers and other relations deflate Teresa's too serious adolescent pretensions. Thus we are made to see Teresa from the outside as well as from within. And at numerous points in the narrative, Christina Stead makes a pointed contrast between Teresa's theoretical knowledge of life, culled from romantic reading and textbooks on psychology, and her actual response to experience, so that again and again our attention is drawn to the fatal gap between Teresa's perception of reality and the true nature of things. One of the major subtleties of this novel arises from the fact that Teresa's greatest weakness and her greatest strength spring ultimately from the same source: her intense romantic imagination. On the one hand, this distorts her understanding of herself and other people, leading her to over-value Jonathan Crow as a young man of genius, to misjudge his intellect and even to mistake two lines of Dr Johnson's poem *The Vanity of Human Wishes* for Jonathan's own, 'This mournful truth is everywhere confessed/ Slow rises worth by poverty depressed.' On the other hand, it is her intense romantic imagination that enables Teresa to reject the circumscribed petty bourgeois world around her, a world of shabby convention, guilt, shame, and repression; a world of smooth-faced hypocrisy, of 'concupiscent fever', a world of sniggering innuendo. For Teresa, the world of books and the boundless world of the sea and sky offer her an alternative, an escape from this materialistic, convention-bound world of Sydney. But we need to note that in such passages as that which describes 'lovers as thick as locusts behind her when she turned into the beach path' (p. 64), what we have is a picture of reality distorted by Teresa's inflamed adolescent imaginings. There are many similar passages. But we are not always certain how to take some passages because of the uncertainty of tone.

Critics looking at the first chapters of the book tend to focus entirely on chapter 3, 'Malfi's Wedding'. Certainly, this is a fine set piece. It combines social comedy with an acute insight into the way in which social rituals expose false values. But in fact this chapter is part of an interlocking system of scenes that portray the perversions and distortions of love produced by the conventions of society. Malfi's wedding is a loveless one and a sham, as appears later. Among the guests, Aunt Di symbolises 'the long night of spinsterdom' (p. 75) that all the young girls fear, while the bawdy, garrulous Aunt Bea revels in the occasion, initiating some into the mysteries of sex and marriage through her broad jokes and crude innuendos, but shocking others and embarrassing her unmarried daughter Ann.

A vital part of the interlocking system is the scene at Aunt Bea's after the wedding, when Teresa discovers Ann crying on the bathroom floor, a pathetic victim of her mother's insistent emphasis on sex and marriage. Providing an ironic background is the intensely religious Mrs Percy – who once went in for Darwinism, free-thinking, and the women's movement' (p. 53), but who is now a victim of neurotic repression and fear; her husband driven mad and in an asylum. Related to this complicated interlocking pattern of ill-directed emotion, frustration and madness, is Teresa's reaction to the 'pale sterility' of her 29-year-old cousin Ellen, to the necking party at the Carlin's house, to the young man struck down by madness when about to be married and the girl still hopelessly in love, and finally Teresa's embarrassed encounter with the exhibitionist on the lonely road. To this complex pattern of distorted love, we need to add the opening battle scene between Teresa and her father, who pours out a mass of contradictions about love and the proper behaviour for a young woman, an outpouring full of self-confession, craving for affection and direct abuse of Teresa for her dowdiness and unde-monstrativeness. Some of Teresa's later inner-contradictions spring from her father's insidious influence, which is for-mally rejected but unconsciously assimilated.

The reader should recognise the cumulative force of these interlocking dramatic scenes, as Stead includes passages that analyse and sum up their significance. She also uses emblematic passages, such as 'What the moon saw' in chapter 6 (pp. 74-5). This sums up woman's fate in a series of images, woman forced into hole-in-the-corner marriages, woman as a 'hunter without a forest', woman made to put out leaves and flowers in such a brief summer. The effect is to reinforce the imprisoning, cyclical structure. Christina Stead is a clumsy, repetitive writer, but the repetitions are mainly functional; they exist to stress the meaningless cycle of existence. Teresa's wide-ranging reflections on the ferry serve a similar function; so also do the syntactic move-ments of the prose from simple past and present tenses to continuitive and participial forms, implying habitual action, long duration, a repetitive circle.

But certainly it is through her dramatic set pieces that Christina Stead communicates her vision most effectively: the initial conflict between father and daughter; the scene at Malfi's wedding; the party at the Carlins'; the farewell scene where Teresa in her rain-drenched cheap stockinette suit looks down at Jonathan's departing ship; and, greatest of them all, the recognition and awakening scene in the deserted sawmill.

> There was a great clattering in the yard as if someone were throwing things about. The floor was trembling with wind. The rain had ceased. With her ear close to the floor, she heard a regular grinding and splashing sound and remembered the sluice-doors left open; the water was pouring in, out of this weather. She sat up. Without a doubt the mill-wheel was turning and shaking the empty building. She took the matches from the ruck-

sack and picked her way to the sluice-gate side of the wheel-chamber, lighting matches several times in the draughts. There was the master of the mill come back to life while they slept. Grinding and groaning, shrieking, it turned downwards into the boiling pool while the timbers tried to rear apart. She went back to Jonathan and said: 'Help me shut the sluice, the wheel is turning.' (p. 407)

At the mill, confronted by something greater and more mysterious than their social selves, Teresa and Jonathan discover their deep dislike of each other. Stead removes the characters from the social world to the elemental. The great hole and black pool are images of the unknown, while the circular movement of the mill wheel and the swift linear onward rush of the waters symbolise the two great organising structures of the novel.

The environment dramatised in the early chapters has two effects on Teresa. It compels her to dissociate herself from it in a series of conscious disengagements that often create surprise and embarrassment for others; but, in the case of her decision to leave the weeping Ann, forces her to realise that Aunt Bea's maternal solicitude for her daughter was more humane than Teresa's own self-righteous detachment. The second effect of this environment is to create false expectations in Teresa herself, so that her ambition to be 'noble, loved, glorious, admired' becomes too narrowly associated with love and marriage, her family seen as 'a family of sleepwalkers waiting to awake through marriage' (p. 86); it also blinds her to Jonathan Crow's inadequacies as a potential liberator and husband.

There is a nice irony in Christina Stead's creation of Crow's character, in that this prophet of free love is in fact a manipulator of others for his own selfish needs: he manipulates the maid, the girls in his study circle, the waitress, and Teresa herself. We first see this 'dark axe-faced, starved young man, with spectacles and a black felt hat' (p. 23) through Kitty's undeluded eyes, just as much later James Quick provides a sharply critical perspective of the man whom Teresa had uncritically admired. 'I see all. The stifled bestiality of the monastery, the crackpot egotism of the cracker-barrel sage' (p. 416). Some readers find Crow wholly repellent and think Teresa must have been a fool not to see through him. In this connection, two points are worth making. Young women should not think of Crow as if he were a real person, a possible or impossible academic lover, and react accordingly. He inhabits a fictional universe; he is almost as much a verbal creation as Zoellner in Murray Bail's short story 'Zoellner's Definition'; he has no existence outside the verbal structure of the novel and this verbal structure makes him a necessary and integral part of the universal quest for power and love. And the second point is that one essential meaning of the novel embodied in its structure is that the youthful quest for love and knowledge can blind a young woman, can limit her perception of reality. One might also add that one of the deeper subtleties of the novel lies in Christina Stead's art of making us see that Crow's compulsive boasting and self-pity have something in common with the character of Teresa's father, Andrew Hawkins, and secondly that Teresa and Crow do in fact have much in common (poverty, lack of confidence, emotional repression, a limited perception of reality), and thirdly that when Teresa at last glories in her new found independence and power to attract men in London she becomes – at least temporarily – a manipulator of other people, like Jonathan Crow. It may be that the image of the beggar and the parasite that immediately precedes her last sight of the 'sliding fumbling' figure of Jonathan Crow as a 'typical self-pickled bachelor' is not only to be linked with Jonathan alone, with his parasitic, vampire-like living off others, but also, more lightly, with herself – and indeed with all of us. The suggestion would be that in even the freest love relationship one of the partners will live parasitically on the other. Certainly, however, Stead sharply differentiates the importance of *will* in each. For Crow, will is a means of dominating others and avoiding moral responsibility; for Teresa, will is a necessary quality to sustain her in her quest.

Teresa finds in James Quick a man who can love generously. It comes as a revelation. It liberates her from the self doubt and masochistic self-laceration she had undergone with Jonathan. But there is still something parasitic in this relation. Quick's attitude becomes possessive like Crow's and threatens Teresa's development as a writer. Teresa compromises her integrity by maintaining comfortable illusions for Quick, who would be hurt by too much reality. She resigns 'herself to playing apart within' in a 'labyrinth of concealment and loving mendacity' (p. 460). Quick is not nearly as rounded and convincing a character as Crow; he is a *deus ex machina* who serves three obvious functions in the structure of the novel: he provides a sharply critical perspective of Crow and thus releases Teresa from her self-delusion and bondage; he provides Teresa's first experience of a generous lover (Crow was capable of entering into sordid intrigue but incapable of generous love, the last thing he wished to give was the gift of love) (p. 197); and, finally, Quick provides Teresa with an introduction into a new world of expanding horizons.

This world expands to admit Harry Girton. Girton is a period stereotype: the shabby Oxford, left-wing graduate of the thirties who sees his political mission in life as fighting for socialism in the Spanish Civil War and his private mission as liberating young women through uninhibited sex. The brief Oxford idyll is described through inflated Lawrentian prose, but Christina Stead's ingrained scepticism breaks through, so that when it is all over Teresa sees the 'immense dusk-white flower' of her love being carried away down the river of time (p. 489). For Teresa, Harry provides the supreme revelation of love and the possibilities of real independence: 'here she found the oracle of her life, this secret deity which is usually sealed from us' (p. 490). And she wonders in a very Blakean fashion, why it is that this 'perfect, absolute joy, is the thing surrounded with "thou shalt not"' (p. 490). This is one of several passages in the novel that can be used to support the claim that Teresa's odyssey is specifically a 'female odyssey', that it ends with a woman's discovery of her independent power to achieve joy. Unsatisfactory as the creation of the Harry Girton episode is in many ways, it does serve the most important function of completing – as far as it can be completed – Teresa's quest. Having discovered her independent capacity for joy in a free relationship, she is content to return to James Quick, knowing that ideals of chastity and monogamy are irrelevant, but that she still loves James Quick.

Of all the critics of this novel only Brian Kiernan, in his book *Images of Society and Nature*, has done justice to the importance of Christina Stead's social preoccupations in this novel. Poverty is a major theme. So too is the effect of a hypocritical materialistic society on personal fulfilment. Crow makes poverty his excuse; Teresa fights against it. It is a great mistake to see Teresa's struggles as purely internal and psychological. Christina Stead was a committed Marxist when she wrote *For Love Alone*, so she was unlikely to neglect economic and social pressures. Like Teresa, she had taught backward children, like Teresa she had worked in a factory to which she walked daily from Circular Quay to save money, and like Teresa she had known the effects of grinding poverty and a circumscribed world. Stead's first novel was a novel about poverty called *The Seven Poor Men of Sydney*. For the seven years of Teresa's life up to May 1936, Christina Stead draws on her own experience of impoverished youth in the early 1920s in Sydney. However, this conflation of two quite different periods produces some confusion. For example, it is extremely unlikely that Teresa would look at a copy of *Vision* with its Norman Lindsay nudes in a tram in the 1930s (p. 209), since *Vision* belonged to Christina Stead's youth in the early 1920s, and copies would already be collectors' items by the 1930s. But the novel does specifically criticise the Nietzschean championing of the will that was characteristic of the magazine *Vision*, doing so through the figure of Crow who thinks of himself as a free spirit 'beyond good and evil' (p. 376). It also criticises that magazine's championing of erotic pleasure and man's dominance in love. The conflation of two periods produces a further anachronism and ambiguity. It is not always apparent that Teresa is living through the Great Depression, because for the most part the cultural and economic ethos of the novel belongs to the early 1920s. And the introduction of the Spanish Civil War is just a convenient fictional device for getting rid of Harry Girton; the War is not lived through as a crucial political challenge.

The surprising thing about Christina Stead's major fiction is the absence of direct political criticism. Even in her study of the Parisian Banking System in *The House of All Nations*, she is more interested in understanding the complexity of the organism (the money market) than with criticising it. Her main motive in writing *For Love Alone* seems to be to communicate her hard-won understanding of the infinitely complex forces, internal and external, that operate when an idealistic young woman looks for joy and fulfilment through the related quest for love, knowledge, equality and independence. If I were asked what does the novel *say*, my answer would run something like this, but first I would have to put an enormous circle round both my diagrams to represent the determining pressures of society.

For Love Alone seems to *say* that if life is an endless quest for love, knowledge and independence (which it probably *is*), then the pattern of this quest is determined, and the possibilities of achievement limited, by two kinds of forces: on the one hand, internal psychological mechanisms that distort perceptions of reality; and, on the other hand, external social pressures like grinding poverty, injustice, inequality between the sexes, which also distort reality. The novel offers an optimistic vision heavily qualified by a philosophy of psychological and social determinism.

NOTES

1. In a radio interview broadcast by the Australian Broadcasting Commission on 24 February 1980.
2. Lionel Trilling, *The Liberal Imagination: Essays on Literature and Society* (Harmondsworth: Penguin, 1970), pp. 72-6.
3. P. 502. All references to *For Love Alone* are to the Pacific Books paperback edition (Melbourne and London: Angus and Robertson, 1966).

Imagery and Structure in Patrick White's Novels

KARIN HANSSON

The general critical background concerning Patrick White's central novels is hardly one of accord. Critics disagree about White's aims, methods, achievement and style. Nor do they agree as to the recommendable method of approaching his fiction. They even discuss whether his novels actually *are* novels, 'wisdom literature' or poetry. Two critical divisions can be illustrated by quoting Professor John Colmer, who in 1978 found that there is no longer need for 'patient exegesis of the figurative patterns in the novels and for detailed charting of the parallels between White's terminology and that of Jung', wishing instead for 'some independent artistic judgement' carried out by critics who devote themselves to 'a detached humanistic analysis of White's sensibility and world-view as embodied in the linguistic texture of his fiction'. Veronica Brady's attitude, on the other hand, is one of fear that 'structural analysis may distort the impact of the work getting between it and the common reader'.[1]

In an attempt at combining critical methods, aiming at what might be called a holographical idea of Patrick White's fictional universe, I have found that the existence of a structural basis, represented by Jung, for example, and a simultaneous dynamic growth and development and continual shifts of point-of-view are not mutually exclusive. The imposition of extrinsic systems does not prevent a concentration on intrinsic artistic achievement. Rather the complexity of White's style and the intricate correspondence of meaning and form seem to demand this double approach. The simultaneous existence of *static* and *dynamic* components can be seen as related to the diagrammatic features of White's literary structures and their recurrent triangles, circles, spheres and quaternities. If we imagine a graphic representation of the organization of the novels, the *horizontal* axis is needed to show how they hang together, how they become gradually enriched by an accumulation of meaning, and how conflicting view-points combine. At the same time we should notice the *vertical* lines which reach down towards underlying layers of biblical and classical knowledge, the traditions of the author's European heritage, and the archetypes of the myths and the human psyche. Both these dimensions, it seems to me, must be employed in an endeavour to suggest the idea of wholeness in White's fictional and metaphysical universe.

To start with the vertical dimension: In a linguistic study Professor Claes Schaar has demonstrated the dynamic function of what he terms 'vertical context systems', involving two stages. 'Recognition means that the surface context, operating as a signal, triggers a memory of the infra-context. Then, as recognition turns to understanding, the signal is transformed into a sign.'[2] The underlying, static contexts thus enrich the surface context by means of 'allusions in the proper sense of the term, overt or covert, and all conceivable borderline cases down to reminiscences and faint echoes of various kinds, quite irrespective of authors' awareness'. This function mainly has a bearing on abstract, religious or philosophical, issues. White's novels abound in contexts which illustrate this kind of *vertical* relation. To a considerable degree his recurrent imagery is composed of sets of signs involved in an infracontextual function, and the parallels with Homer, the Bible, Jung, Shakespeare,

Blake, Schopenhauer and others could preferably be regarded from this point of view. When White, as he often does, relies on the Jungian language of archetype, this achieves its effect through a set of key metaphors working under the surface of rational verbalization, embodying spiritual status. This is indirectly corroborated by the author himself who says: 'I have the same idea with all my books; an attempt to come close to the core of reality, the structure of reality, as opposed to the merely superficial.'[3]

Connections between meaning and form, between style and theme, could by preference be illustrated and analysed with the structuralist method based on the function of 'foregrounded' elements, as represented by the Czech scholar Jan Mukařovský. Such components, which in different ways cause a stylistic break or distortion, deviate from expected patterns, bring about a thematic twist, or in some other ways make a phrase or a passage stand out in relief against the background, constitute a dynamic relationship with less foregrounded elements in White's prose. The function of relativity, contrast and hierarchy is significant because of the multidimensional and polydynamic character of White's manner of writing. As Mukařovský puts it: 'the structure is revealed as a concert of forces.'[4] Within the series of novels the foregrounding of certain abstractions like suffering, humility, knowledge and nakedness is perceptible. Spiritually heightened moments, or 'epiphanies', are brought into prominence. Foregrounding components can also consist of striking repetitions of phrases and words, obvious changes in style and atmosphere, recurring elements and recognizable patterns. White's much criticized peculiarities of punctuation, sentence structure and wording have the same kind of effect.

This method implies a flexible and functional approach and regards the literary work as a coherent whole, consisting of interacting components, a system of signs. When Cecil Hadgraft points out that the whole of *The Tree of*

Man 'is an elaboration of significances, not so much of relations between people ... as of relations between a person and the physical world',[5] and notices that 'countless details, which for us all are normally trivial, are subtly and momentarily made complex', this suggests the foregrounding effect as a stylistic device to emphasize the metaphysical aspects as well as the lack of normal (and verbal) communication between White's protagonists and their surrounding communities. At the same time it is indicative of their peculiar faculty of response to significant details of physical reality.

It is possible to discern in White's novels what might be called 'a unity of mystery'. It would lead too far, however, to exemplify the metaphysical and psychological backgrounds shared by all the novels, but Jung, though important, is certainly not the only source of White's figurative patterns and images. To discuss the archetypal character of his spiritual universe, the recurrent dualistic arrangements, the relationship between man and God, the function of the arts, the boundaries of human will-power, the necessity of suffering and humiliation and other recurrent themes, a consideration of the affinities between White and writers and theoreticians like Jung, Blake, Buber, Schopenhauer, Meister Eckhart and others is profitable and relevant. White's use of epigraphs, allusions or signals integrated in the narrative surface context often suggests such vertical, infracontextual connections. At times, though, a gap can be perceived between meaning and form, between what White obviously wants to say and what he actually achieves. This also affects credibility. White has often been accused of not being explicit and of deficiencies in credibility, which probably to a large extent can be explained by his elaborate use of infracontexts. The reader must be sensitive to the signals provided, prepared for a momentary switch between a realistic and a symbolic mode of interpretation. The complex structures do not admit of questions like Leonie Kramer's '...if Mrs Godbold's saucepans are sacred, what is wrong with Mrs Rosetree's mixmaster?'[6] Hurtle Duffield's vision of the Indigo and Elizabeth Hunter's experience of the storm belong to the events the reader must acquiesce in, unconditionally, or the novels fall flat. Verisimilitude and logical argumentation can, consequently, not always be expected.

On the *horizontal* plane the recurrence of certain symbols, which grow, interact and form significant image clusters and certain key abstractions, which also tend to form clusters, ought to be noticed because White's message to a large extent is conveyed through imagery and structure rather than by the plot. By such means elements and associations are carried over from one novel to another, and a characteristic cumulative effect is achieved. *The Aunt's Story* provides the embryos of the most prominent image clusters, composed of the Garden, the Rose, the Tree and the House. Each image, to use Northrop Frye's vocabulary, is both apocalyptic and demonic, an attribute of redemption or destruction, and these images throughout the series of books gradually deepen and develop, interact and fuse. Also in the early novels we can discern the embryos of the central images of the middle novels, *Voss, Riders in the Chariot*, and *The Solid Mandala*, that is the Desert, the Chariot and the Mandala related to the characteristic idea of the spiritual journey or quest, the typical contrast of the indigenous and the foreign, of Australia and Europe, of nature and society, together with the mandalic notions connected with the circle, the centre, the quaternity and the blue colour. The recognition of the signal function of these elements considerably facilitates the interpretation of each novel when seen against the background of its predecessors.

Similarly when the key abstractions tend to form clusters these suggest metaphysical and spiritual modes of interpretation. Thus the idea of wholeness and unity as opposed to dividedness and fragmentation is largely brought to the fore by means of imagery of stones, sand, glass fragments, jewels, splinters, sticks and chips. The more religiously orientated the novel, the more prominent this type of imagery appears to be, and in the books succeeding *The Eye of the Storm* the typical clusters no longer occur, hardly even the single images, a fact which suggests a shift of thematic emphasis in White's fiction. The three middle novels, *Voss*, *Riders in the Chariot* and *The Solid Mandala*, contain the most elaborate use of image clusters and of geometric structures which also suggests their 'religious' character. Just as the fusion of garden, tree and house, which can be illustrated by Mary Hare's diningroom at Xanadu, Hurtle Duffield's dunny and conservatory, and Glastonbury in *The Tree of Man*, works as a signal for the reader, the key abstraction of knowledge, simplicity, nakedness, freedom etc. tend to fuse, and a foregrounding effect is brought about by their striking recurrence in almost formulary phraseology, by their appearance in climactic moments, by syntactic breaks, stylistic changes and clashes and by their connections with White's spiritual seekers exclusively. Knowledge in White's wording approaches the purport of illumination, and the urge to obtain this total all-embracing knowledge and the willingness to accept its consequences are expressed by those characters we refer to as White's questers. Links between them are established regardless of differences on the narrative level, by a style approaching formula as the following quotations exemplify.

'I would like to know,' said Theodora. 'I would like to know everything.' (*The Aunt's Story*, p. 39)

I study everything. I want to do everything. (*The Tree of Man*, p. 327)

Knowing so much, I shall know everything, [Voss] assured himself... (*Voss*, p. 27)

I shan't feel happy till I've tasted everything there is to taste and I don't intend to refuse what is unpleasant – that is experience of another kind. (*The Eye of the Storm*, p. 351)[7]

Thus on the horizontal plane the novels can be likened to an intricate weft in which a number of threads of special colours and textures recombine into continually new patterns and motives. It is evident that they serve as components of a motif which all White's central novels have in common: the solitary individual's search for ultimate insight and fulfilment. Whether the narration deals with the growing neurosis of a spinster, and expedition into the Australian desert or the death of an old woman in modern Sydney these threads connect each single novel with all the others.

To sum up: The horizontal and the vertical connections are equally important in the study of Patrick White's fictional universe. To come to grips with the complexities of his style, his methods and his themes both dimensions are to be taken into account.

NOTES

1. R. Shepherd and K. Singh, eds., *Patrick White: A Critical Symposium* (Adelaide, 1978), pp. 136 and 139 respectively.
2. Claes Schaar, *The Full Voic'd Quire Below: Vertical Context Systems in 'Paradise Lost'*. Lund Studies in English 60 (Lund: Gleerup, 1982), p. 18.
3. Interview with Patrick White in Craig McGregor et al., *In the Making* (Melbourne, 1969), quoted from John Docker, 'Patrick White and Romanticism: *The Vivisector*', *Southerly* Vol. 33 (1973), 46.
4. Jan Mukařovsk , 'Standard Language and Poetic Language' in *A Prague School Reader on Esthetics, Literary Structure and Style*, transl. P.L. Garvin (Wasington D.C., 1958); reprinted in Chatham and Levin, eds., *Essays on the Language of Literature* (Boston, 1967).
5. Cecil Hadgraft, 'The Theme of Revelation in Patrick White's Novels', *Southerly* Vol. 37 (1977), 37.
6. Leonie Kramer, 'Patrick White's Götterdämmerung', *Quadrant*, June 1973, 18.
7. The references to Patrick White's novels are to the Penguin editions.

Patrick White:
An International Perspective

JOHN COLMER

During the last thirty years there has been a great upsurge of creative activity in Australia and the major achievements of Australian writers, painters, musicians, and film makers are now internationally recognized. It is over ten years since Patrick White was awarded a Nobel Prize for literature. More recently, Thomas Keneally won the highly coveted Booker Prize for his novel *Schindler's Ark*. And the recent death of Christina Stead marked the passing of a Marxist writer whose towering genius was recognized throughout the world. The work of such younger writers as Randolph Stow, David Malouf and David Ireland is now well known in Europe. And at least one of the 'new wave' dramatists, David Williamson, is highly valued outside Australia, for his film script of *Gallipoli*, if not for his controversial plays, *The Club* and *The Department*.

This great upsurge of creative activity should be seen against a wider background of cultural change which has been brought about by massive post-war immigration, increased government funding of the arts and the creation of large Arts Centres and Arts Festivals in all the major cities. The achievements in literature also need to be linked with the great renaissance in painting that began in the early

1950s. Such painters as Russell Drysdale and Sidney Nolan enabled Australians to see their national myths and their landscape with new eyes. Nolan's series of paintings on the bushranger Ned Kelly and his series on Gallipoli are the most obvious examples of this radical reinterpretation of national myths. At a time when the British and American cultural traditions seem tired and played out, the art and literature of Australia appeal to young people everywhere as having a force, a freshness and a vitality to be found nowhere else, except in certain West Indian, African and European writers. For the serious literary critic the appeal is rather different: Australian literature offers a challenging example of the way a transplanted culture has been radically transposed in a relatively brief historical period.

The greatest figure in the Australian cultural scene is undoubtedly Patrick White – much loved, much hated, still a highly controversial figure, and still in need of objective assessment. I hope to have provided such an assessment in the book I have just completed and on which I draw from time to time in this paper.[1] To place Patrick White in an international perspective and to illustrate the rival claims of Europe and Australia on his imagination, I am going to divide my talk into three parts: 1) Patrick White and Europe; 2) Patrick White and Australia; and 3) Patrick White and the critics. But first just let me remind you that White is the author of eleven massive novels, seven plays, two collections of short stories, and a revealing work of autobiography, *Flaws in the Glass*, published only recently. Now seventy-two years old, he does not plan to write any more novels, but, as he told me in a letter recently, is experimenting with writing words for music, possibly an opera. For a life-long victim of ill-health, Patrick White provides an astonishing example of sustained creative energy and fresh experiment.

Patrick White is a giant among the moderns. He offers a completely new experience to readers mainly familiar with the recent British novel. They will have encountered little that is comparable to his grand archetypal themes and grotesque modes, except perhaps in the epic scale and metaphysical panorama of painter-novelists like Wyndham Lewis and Mervyn Peake. Patrick White is himself a frustrated painter and musician. He speaks in an autobiographical essay, 'The Prodigal Son', of wishing to produce in his fiction 'the textures of music, the sensuousness of paint ... what Delacroix and Blake might have seen, what Mahler and Liszt may have heard'. From such a novelist, we cannot therefore expect the social realism and decent liberal morality of the British tradition, or the formal experimentation and extreme self-consciousness of the post-modernist American novel. His mentors are Dickens, Dostoevsky and Melville. His mammoth fictions possess the amplitude of theme and profusion of detail of the great nineteenth-century novel, combined with stream-of-consciousness techniques associated with James Joyce, Virginia Woolf and William Faulkner. He also owes a general debt to European Expressionism, which taught him the value of grotesque and distorted forms for expressing the irrational in human nature. Yet, in spite of such obvious debts, he has created a wholly individual kind of novel. Few modern writers have found more varied ways of dramatising the dynamic tension between inner and outer worlds or of exploring the quest for meaning in an apparently meaningless universe. He has also created a highly personal style, so that almost any page bears the unmistakable signature of his total world view. His vision is both eclectic and eccentric. It has much in common with the social and moral paradoxes that underlie Blake's poetry, and owes much, as the epigraphs make clear, to the pioneer thinkers of the modern tradition, ranging from Mahatma Ghandi to Paul Eluard. His major novels, unlike so much sceptical recent fiction, move inexorably towards some grand positive affirmation about life.

Patrick White and Europe

From the start it is important to recognise White's conflicting loyalties to Europe and Australia. He was born in London in 1912 when his wealthy parents were on an extended honeymoon. They belonged to the Australian class which educated its sons at English public schools and at Oxford and Cambridge, spent long periods in Europe, rented English country houses and Mediterranean villas, lived a patrician, privileged life, and owned vast sheep properties the size of a large English county. White's father gave him a generous allowance that set him free to travel widely in Europe and America and to become a writer. He was nearly forty when he returned to settle in Australia and the land he returned to in 1948 was very different from the one he left in the inter-war years. Politically and economically it was no longer so dependent on England, the 'home' country; culturally, it was developing vigorous national traditions, especially through the expressionist paintings of Drysdale and Nolan, two artists with whom White shared a revitalised image of the vastness and mystery of the Australian Outback. But, to White's horror and dismay, the increased prosperity and independence seemed to exacerbate the materialism, philistinism and tasteless gentility of Australian suburban culture. Europe and Australia, the beauty of the landscape and the philistinism of the suburbs – these are the poles between which White's fiction moves.

White is now internationally famous. Books on his work have been published in Australia, Britain, Canada and Sweden.[2] Faced with such a formidably difficult writer, critics have naturally concentrated on patient exegesis. They have also paid tribute to his genius – formally recognised by the award of a Nobel Prize in 1973. But there has been little attempt at evaluating the individual works or seeing the connection between White the dramatist and White the novelist. My own book will stress the dramatic tensions in White between the frustrated actor and the self-conscious dreamer, between the artist who lives through others and the solitary gazer into the distorting mirrors of the self.

White's works are rooted in the painful drama of his early life. In his autobiography he writes: 'In the theatre of my imagination I should say there are three or four basic sets, all of them linked to the actual past, which can be dismantled and re-constructed to accommodate the illusion of reality life boils down to.'[3] Most of the sets combine a symbolic house, distorting mirrors, wild garden and a privileged visionary whose life has been moulded by an ineffective father and a dominating mother. But because everything he has written has been 'dredged up from the unconscious', the transposition of life into art has been a rich and complex affair. Over and over again, White has insisted that he is not a realistic writer, nor an intellectual one, nor a moralist who 'preaches sermons' in his books. Nevertheless, it is true that his central moral and imaginative preoccupation has been to discover a unity that would transcend the obvious dualities of existence. In his seventies, however, he seems to have become reconciled to a limited achievement both in life and art. Sadly, he confesses: 'The ultimate spiritual union is probably as impossible to achieve as the perfect work of art or the unflawed human relationship. In matters of faith, art, and love I have had to reconcile myself to starting again where I began.'[4]

He began early. He wrote a play, *The Mexican Bandits* (1921), when he was nine, a piece of romantic fiction a few years later, and three novels ('more honest in their lumbering truth than my subsequent chase after a fashionable style in London')[5] when as a young man he worked for two years on the land learning the practical skills of farming.

His first published story, 'The Twitching Colonel', printed in 1937, is a strange story about a retired colonel who had once seen the Indian rope trick performed in India. It presents a type of experience that is to recur in much of White's later fiction. The story is structured on the contrast between two views of reality and two responses to life: the mystic and the materialistic. As in White's later works, the privileged visionary figure – in this case the eccentric colonel – is placed against a background of jeering uncomprehending people; he is a figure of fun for the boys in the London streets. Also, as in the later fiction, the moment of vision comes from a return to the past, the memory of a mystic moment in India. And this memory coincides with the moment of death. The London fire in which the colonel dies is a symbol of the heightened consciousness that combines personal extinction and the perception of the unity of all things. Similar fires and similar visionary moments recur frequently in White's work. All White's later fiction turns on the distinction made in this short story between external appearance and internal reality, between surface meaning and underlying significance. Through the creation of this duality he invests the physical world with spiritual values. His characters discover the world of the spirit in and through the material world, and some immersion in evil – it is suggested – is necessary to achieve the highest good.

White's first novel, *Happy Valley*, published in 1939, also explores the lonely quest for truth in an alien, materialistic world. But in this case there is no apocalyptic climax for the central character, but rather a passive acceptance of the spiritual value of suffering. At the end, the hero discovers that he 'is immune from all but the ultimate destruction of the inessential outer shell'. From this point onwards, White's fiction explores the process by which people discover the core of reality within the inessential outer shell, both of themselves and the natural world. The second apprentice novel, *The Living and the Dead*, published in 1941, moves from the philosophical acceptance of suffering to weary resignation and despair. This very English novel charts the same kind of experience as T.S. Eliot's *The Waste Land*, but it also explores the idea of political commitment as a possible salvation for the half-alive inhabitants of London in the 1930s. Thus, two of the characters go off to fight against Franco in the Spanish Civil War.

The third of the novels written during White's long stay in Europe is a masterpiece. *The Aunt's Story*, published in 1948, differs from all his later work in its brevity, its classic simplicity of form and its total lack of strain. The heroine's quest takes her from the apparently secure but far from innocent world of an Australian childhood to the neurotic and divided world of cruelty and passion in pre-war Europe, and finally to a vision of truth and unity in rural America. The ideal of a wise passivity, first celebrated in the novel *Happy Valley*, now acquires a deeper meaning as the heroine learns to 'accept the irreconcilable halves' of her being. Yet there is something perverse in the idea that only by being condemned as mad can the heroine reach final sanity of vision. This is a paradox that White continues to assert throughout his works. The total rejection of society that White's ending implies is completely in line with his later celebration of the sanity of his misunderstood solitaries and the insanity of the world, a celebration that reaches its logical conclusion in his last play *Netherwood* (1983), where he dramatises the conflicting values in a grand shoot-out between the representatives of a 'mad' society and the 'sane' patients in a private mental home.

The early novels I have discussed so far illustrate the fictional matrix from which all White's works spring. Its major constituents are a belief in visionary experience and the redemptive power of love, an almost compulsive return to childhood experiences for illuminations and epiphanies, the creative exercise of memory, fragmentation as a necessary prelude to psychic harmony, ironic reversal of orthodox ideas of success and failure, sanity and madness; and, underlying all these, the lonely quest for truth, the core of being, which is hidden beneath the surface. In spite of the strong personal elements in this fictional matrix the novels cannot, however, be called autobiographical. The process by which White fragments his personality to live through the most unlikely characters makes it difficult for the reader to enjoy any easy identification with a privileged central figure, even in *The Aunt's Story*, and quite impossible in the later novel *The Solid Mandala*, where he lives through the strongly contrasted twin brothers with equal imaginative intensity. The author's self is reflected and refracted in each novel as a whole, not in a single figure.

Patrick White and Australia

After nearly forty years in Europe White returned to live permanently in Australia in 1948. This marked the main turning point in his career. He has described how one day on his small farm outside Sydney he fell on his back in the mud and knew that God had struck – just as he strikes so many of Patrick White's specially privileged characters. From now on the religious impetus in his fiction was strong. The return also led to a changed conception of writing. 'Writing,' he explains, 'which had meant for him the practice of an art by a polished mind in civilised surroundings, became a struggle to create completely fresh forms out of rocks and sticks of words.' From now on, White wrote about strange visionary characters in an Australian setting. These later novels form themselves naturally into three groups: first, Australian epics; second, the visions of inspired artists; and third, the visions of the ordinary ones.

The first result of White's return was the publication of two Australian epics, *The Tree of Man* (1955) and *Voss* (1957). His motives in coming back included a 'longing to return to the scenes of childhood ... the purest well from which the creative artist draws', 'a nostalgia for the desert landscape' of Australia, and a determination to escape the sterile fate of becoming a London intellectual. But at first he was appalled by the intellectual emptiness, the march of material ugliness and the 'exaltation of the average'. He therefore wrote *The Tree of Man*, a story of a simple pioneering couple in the Australian Bush, to reveal 'the extraordinary behind the ordinary, the mystery and poetry which alone could make bearable the lives of such people' and, incidentally, his own life since his return.

These two Australian epics, *The Tree of Man* and *Voss*, are both based on the metaphor of life seen as a journey, a favourite metaphor in much Australian writing for obvious historical and geographical reasons. In *The Tree of Man* the hero, Stan Parker's journey is through time; in *Voss* the hero's journey is through space. But in both novels, the temporal and spatial voyages are in essence spiritual ones. At the moment of death, Stan Parker is granted a vision of God. The insanely proud Voss, on the other hand, who is a Nietzschean hero, knows that God is dead, and seeks to fill the void by becoming a god himself. In both novels, White's desire to break away from the kind of Australian fiction that was, 'the dreary dun-coloured offspring of journalistic realism and give his prose 'the textures of music, the sensuousness of paint' is triumphantly realised.

The next group of novels, *Riders in the Chariot* (1961), *The Solid Mandala* (1961) and *The Vivisector* (1970) are all in the form of extended metaphors and all focus on the transfiguring experiences of lonely visionaries and artists. They are concerned with establishing the supremacy of feeling over intellect and with establishing the connection between suffering and spiritual insight. The artist figure gradually assumes a more important role. In *Riders in the Chariot*, an Aboriginal artist's paintings mediate the significance of a Jewish refugee's mock crucifixion and death; in *The Solid Mandala*, one of the two main characters possesses the artist's seeing eye; and, in *The Vivisector*, Patrick White places the artist figure, Hurtle Duffield, in the centre of the fictional world and explores the implications of the idea of the artist as both creator and justified destroyer. Of these figures Alf Dubbo, the Aboriginal artist, offers an interesting example of the strains involved when a white Anglo-Saxon writer attempts to inhabit the consciousness of an Aboriginal character. The text reveals unresolved contradictions, especially in the process whereby a socially exploited and alienated Aboriginal is assimilated to the Romantic stereotype of the doomed and accursed artist as represented and defined by Rimbaud.

A second important feature of this group of novels is White's growing disenchantment with Australian suburbia and its false materialistic values. His fictional name for all the composite horrors of Australian suburbia is Sarsaparilla. In one of his plays, called *The Season at Sarsaparilla*, he creates a marvellous expressionist drama to contrast the deadening rhythms of suburbia with the life-giving rhythms of nature. It is not surprising that the comfortable bourgeoisie thoroughly dislike White for his attacks on their values and his celebration of lonely social outcasts.

In the final group of novels, *The Eye of the Storm* (1973), *A Fringe of Leaves* (1976) and *The Twyborn Affair* (1979), White has turned from the visions of artists and alienated visionaries to the visions of common humanity. With this change has come a more compassionate view of human weakness and frailty. *The Eye of the Storm*, which describes the dying moments of a selfish and passionate old woman who experiences a moment of truth on her deathbed, marks a distinct movement away from the abnormal psychology of *The Vivisector* to more ordinary modes of being. This movement is carried a stage further in the novel *A Fringe of Leaves*, whose nineteenth-century heroine is shipwrecked, is initiated into cannibalistic rituals by Aborigines, rescued by an escaped convict and is finally returned to polite society. She thus passes through a series of experiences that enact mankind's evolution from primitive hunter and food-gatherer to civilized human being. Moreover, her identification with the Aborigines after the shipwreck and with her convict rescuer brings this story into relationship with two of the master themes in Australian fiction and Australian history: the attitude of the white colonizers to the Aboriginal people and the harsh treatment of the convicts transported from England to the new colony. The heroine reaches the summit of wisdom when she asserts 'no-one is to blame, and everybody, for whatever happens'. This is the first of White's novels in which the lonely alienated character is wholly reintegrated into the fabric of society at the conclusion.

The reintegration that takes place at the end of his last novel *The Twyborn Affair* is both social and psychological, both public and personal. In the person of the protagonist the novelist dramatises different elements in his own deeply fragmented character. In the first part of the novel, the protagonist appears as a beautiful woman, in the second as a young trainee farmer on a large Australian estate, and in the third as the madame of a fashionable London brothel. In two respects, this novel completed White's development as a novelist. For the first time, the master themes of choice and sexual identity are explicitly related to homosexuality and the ambiguity of sexual roles. The novel as a whole exemplifies the statement that 'true friendship ... if there is anything wholly true – certainly in friendship – comes, I'd say, from the woman in a man and the man in a woman' (p. 360). The second respect in which this novel completes White's development lies in its final resolution of the mother/son relationship that in real life was a source of pain and anguish. At the end of *The Twyborn Affair*, the protagonist is reunited with his mother and accepts the duty of fighting for his country. More and more in recent years White has taken an active role in politics, issuing warning about nuclear war and supporting conservationist issues.

White and the Critics

It is not unusual for a highly original artist to be under-valued or misunderstood by his contemporaries. In fact, Patrick White's works have been highly praised from the start, both in Australia and overseas: yet the novelist him-self has perpetuated the myth of misunderstanding and neglect. Why should this be?

It is, I suggest, a necessary stance, completely in line with White's championing of the despised and defeated in his novels. He identifies so closely with the Romantic tradition of the lone visionary that critics, academics and the general public are necessarily seen as hostile and un-comprehending. Such an attitude is actually inscribed in the texts of his novels, in the neglect of Alf Dubbo's apocalyptic paintings and in the critics' hostility to Hurtle Duffield's disturbing art. Patrick White's outbursts against critics and academics have become *more* not *less* intemper-ate with the passage of time. This is a situation to under-stand rather than deplore. As a non-cerebral writer who has always drawn deeply on the unconscious, White has a natural antipathy towards those who intellectualise art; and inevitably the volume of academic criticism has sharp-ly increased with his growing fame. Like many writers, he is particularly sensitive to tactless enquiries about work in progress. His antipathy to the academic process of canon-ising texts is neatly illustrated by his disparaging remarks about *Voss* now that it has been canonised and made the subject of repeated academic analysis. He sees very clear-ly that the heavy hand of academicism not only destroys the life of the text but substitutes something altogether safer and less challenging. Yet he retains a passionate be-lief in the power of books to change the world and be-lieves that his best books are *The Aunt's Story*, *The Solid Mandala* and *The Twyborn Affair*.

Amid all the diversity of critical opinions about White's work it is possible to isolate some of the more important strands. Liberal humanist critics like William Walsh, by stressing the combination of moral passion and intense imaginative power in White, have had little difficulty in placing his works within the English 'Great Tradition'. Such a placing is seen by others as inappropriate and limiting, since it does little justice to all the non-realistic elements in his fiction; it is better, they suggest, to think of his novels in relation to such great American writers as Hawthorne or Melville, or in relation to the Russian novelist Dostoevsky. A third school of criticism insists that Patrick White has created a fictional genre of his own and that the works must be judged on their own terms and without relation to other forms and traditions. A more hard-headed and sceptical group, typified by Leonie Kramer, has concentrated on what is seen as a gap between intention and achievement in White, and has argued that very frequently the detailed texture of the work generates meanings that run counter to the overt intention embodied in the grand archetypal structure.

White's relations with his readers are as uneasy as those with his critics. In spite of his statement that he writes only for himself and has 'never thought about readership', the texts presuppose and to some extent create two kinds of reader, the one literal-minded and obtuse who needs to be bullied, prodded and cajoled into seeing all the links in the grand design, the other intelligent, sensitive and imaginative, able to grasp the deeper significances of the text. This enormously complicates the reading process; only in the perfectly modulated *The Aunt's Story* does White combine extreme originality with a relaxed confidence in his reader's sensitivity. In the works written after his return to Australia in 1948, the awkward tonal shifts create a sense of strain. This loss of confidence is understandable when it is remembered that his attempts to create a prose to 'convey a splendour, a translucence' in *The Tree of Man* were described by a leading poet and critic, A.D. Hope, as 'pretentious verbal sludge'. Allied to this loss of confidence was his growing disenchantment with Australian culture and suburban life. It is not surprising if at times the reader seems to be equated with the obtuse denizens of Sarsaparilla, implicitly identified with the dullest characters in White's suburban worlds.

White's adversary type of art is inimical to orthodox criticism and to the established social order. Presumably it was the socially subversive elements as well as the visionary ones that first attracted him to European expressionism and surrealism. His own art, which has almost nothing in common with recent post-modernist fiction, has developed its own expressionist and surrealist techniques to explore the quest for truth in a grossly materialistic society. The early works chart the unresolved tensions between the individual and society as the characters pursue the paths of solitude, isolation and individual vision; the middle novels celebrate the powers of the privileged artist to reach truth – and White is quite dogmatic in saying 'I think the artist is privileged'; the last three novels suggest that some kind of reintegration into society is possible for the lonely, spiritually elect. This new vision of a potential reconciliation between the alienated individual and social groups is accompanied by an altogether more compassionate view of human nature. White has finally reaped the rewards of his uncompromising honesty and integrity as an artist and a man.

* Patrick White died on 30 September 1990.

NOTES

1. John Colmer, *Patrick White* (London and New York: Methuen, 1984).
2. At least three books have been published in Sweden since the award of the Nobel Prize in 1973. These are by Ingmar Björk-stén, Mari-Ann Berg and Karin Hansson.

3. Patrick White, *Flaws in the Glass: A Self-Portrait* (Harmondsworth: Penguin, 1983), p. 154. All later references are to Penguin editions of White's works.
4. Ibid., p. 74.
5. Ibid., p. 52.

Vicki Raymond

GOAT SONG

Below Mycenae, on a day of showers,
women were picking olives from the ground.
Two goats were tethered near the road: she, small
with pointed ears; and he, a flop-eared breed
with crooked back. They balanced on one wall,
and nosed each other.

                        Now, the fatal Queen
had beacons placed on every hill and cape
from Hellespont to Sounion; so, when Troy fell,
she, pacing the well-built Mycenaean walls,
cried to the house of Atreus, 'Rejoice!'

Sometimes the plough turns up an arrow head.
Sometimes a she-goat smiles with human eyes.

FROST POCKET

'This house was built in a frost pocket:
we never get the sun.'
I examine the narrow garden
of ferns and moss,
remarking that it must be cool in summer.
'Yes, but we go away then.'

The first owner, the convict, planted
the spuds of freedom here,
but nothing prospered. Squalid
as a cell, the dark yard
sweated a plague of slugs that plopped all night
in his back-broken sleep.

So they have paved it, so they have hung
baskets in the dank air,
trained climbers to seek out the light.
But in the end
you can only shut the gate on it, and take
the whizzing highway to elsewhere.

THE PROFESSIONS OF POETS

For all our talk of 'making',
it isn't an accident
that most poets are either
teachers or bureaucrats.

For teaching, like it or not,
and setting things in order
are closer to poetry
than building walls and weaving.

But we are work-fetishists!
Show us a billbook or scythe,
and we finger it with words.
We call our meetings 'workshops'

because they produce sawdust.
When the window-cleaners come
to our office or schoolroom,
we gaze with envy and lust

(which amount to the same thing)
at men who arrive in vans,
who whistle and wear old clothes,
who are not afraid of heights.

Poets, be tireless teachers!
Don't be afraid of that child
whose father owns the city,
or snub the one with headlice.

Be unbribed bureaucrats too!
Keep your records up to date;
miss nothing that happens;
remember the auditor.

EVER AFTER

You cannot see the bruise –
it's hidden by the ruff –
yet frightened eyes dart hints
of frequent pinch and cuff
such as harsh step-dames use.
That's what excites the prince.

Her clumsiness, to slip
her foot from its white furs –
how promising that seems!
The prince in princely dreams
chews at his underlip,
which he imagines hers.

Years later, when the knocks
have faded, and the court
knows how her lord has strayed,
she'll waste an hour of thought
on old shoes in a box –
then slap her scullery maid.

GREEN IDEAS SLEEP FURIOUSLY

In Plato-land the nurses cross
the silent wards where, it is said,
ideas in rows sleep peacefully,
awaiting their own birth –

except the green ones. See them toss,
as though the sea were in the bed!
Why do they sleep so furiously?
They dream of spring on earth.

Survival, Reincarnation, *Palace of the Peacock* – Attitudes to Death and Life in Commonwealth Literature

BRITTA OLINDER

'What is it that we all know is going to happen but we don't know when or how?'[1] This is Mr Scobie's innocent question in a novel by Australian writer Elizabeth Jolley called *Mr Scobie's Riddle*. The riddle was only meant to be amusing, Mr Scobie says, well, 'thought provoking of course but mostly for amusement' (p. 126). All the same it caused a reaction of horror in the Matron of the nursing home where death, while being taken advantage of as a source of income, is never mentioned and patients even quite recently dead are never spoken of – they 'simply ceased to need to be cared for ... as if they had never existed' (p. 172). In spite of the lugubrious riddle, the novel is, in fact, a farcical, sometimes hilarious story of an institution where the old people are treated at best like children but mostly like recalcitrant animals or objects. In the middle of ageing and dying, however, there is the vitality of some of the inmates in spite of all and, especially, of the young girls cleaning the place, singing and dancing about. And the novel does not end with Mr

Scobie's death but goes on – like life – with new admissions in Mr Scobie's place and with the new-born baby, the daughter of one of the serving girls and Mr Scobie's nephew. There is even an insane old woman's dance in celebration of the new life (p. 211) and her conviction that there is no point in living unless you are doing something towards the future (p. 221).

This is an Australian example of the treatment of life and death. The theme is so wide that it can be said to include practically everything on earth of human interest. In this context, however, it has been taken in the sense of clashes between these opposites, of situations where life and death meet and merge or of life seen in the light of death and vice versa. In English literature we can think of some examples picked at random like the Metaphysical poets speaking of love in terms of death as well as the other way round; the re-interpretation of life in terms of death in Gray's 'Elegy Written in a Country Churchyard'; the constant presence of death in Dylan Thomas's poems; or the total reversal of values as, in the Northern Irish situation, Seamus Heaney asks: 'Is there a life before death?'

One question to consider would be: Is there a difference in the attitudes to these concepts and the treatment of them if we compare Western literature, by which I mean European and American, with Commonwealth literature? And is there a difference between Commonwealth regions? What I propose to do is to give some glimpses from Canada, Australia and New Zealand, countries with a European-based majority and hence presumably with views of life and death fairly close to ours, and then proceed to some instances from India and Africa ending up with a West Indian case. I will use examples that are fairly obvious and could easily be accommodated within a term-length course in Commonwealth Literature.

Let us look, then, at Canadian literature, first through Margaret Atwood's eyes. Her point of departure in her analysis of the writing of her own country, entitled *Survival*, is taking the single, unifying and informing symbol of the United States to be 'the Frontier', the idea of expanding and conquering new territories whether it means going further west or the interest is directed towards the rest of the world or, again, into outer space. In the same way, she argues, the central symbol of Canada is *survival* – like the Frontier a variable and adaptable idea. I will not here go into the term of survival as used by Northrop Frye nor into its validity generally but keep to Atwood's line of argument.[2] She distinguishes between the 'bare survival' of the first explorers and settlers fighting hostile elements to be able to keep alive, that is survival in the sense of living on the borderline between life and death. This is distinguished from the 'grim survival' of a crisis or disaster, like a hurricane or a wreck in which others succumb. Yet another meaning is the 'cultural' survival as applied to French Canada under English dominance or to the original native population or, again, to the whole mixed population of Canada under the commercial and industrial threat from the United States.

Atwood stresses the idea of *hanging on*, of just staying alive:

> ... tales not of those who *made it*, but of those who made it *back* from the awful experience – the North, the snowstorm, the sinking ship – that killed everyone else. The survivor has no triumph or victory but just the fact of his survival; he has little after his ordeal that he did not have before, except gratitude for having escaped with his life.[3]

One example that Atwood presents is E.J. Pratt (1882-1964), the 'popular and dynamic narrative poet who chose big themes of suspended action – a whale hunt, the destruction of a liner by an iceberg, war, martyrdom, the building of a railway' and who focused on 'conflicts between man and nature'. His poem *The Titanic* (1935) is thus 'not only about that liner's ill-fated voyage but about its enemy, an iceberg, and the conduct of its proud, complacent, heroic passengers', most of whom drown. Another of his poems mentioned by Atwood is *Brébeuf and His Brethren* (1940), a twelve-part epic on the seventeenth century Jesuit missions to the Huron Indians, which is climaxed, after crushing ordeals, by the torture and burning of Father Brébeuf and Father Lalemant (1649).

Margaret Laurence's (1926-1987) *The Stone Angel* (1964) is also used to illustrate Atwood's thesis. It is about an old woman who 'hangs grimly on to life but dies at the end'. Another critic has significantly described this character as 'the dominating force in this remarkable book ... a woman large as life who sometimes seems almost the equal of death itself'.[4]

A third writer chosen by Atwood to support her idea of survival is Sinclair Ross (b. 1908). *As for Me and My House* (1941) is 'the story of a frustrated artist who is serving as a minister (although he has no faith) in a succession of poor prairie communities'. He 'hates his job and has crippled himself artistically'.[5] 'It is one of the saddest and most disenchanted of North American novels, yet its influence on other Canadian writers from the West – Margaret Laurence, for example – has been very great.' Margaret Laurence herself says: 'Despite the sombre tone and the dark themes of Sinclair Ross's (short) stories, man emerges as a creature who can survive – and survive with some remaining dignity – against both outer and inner odds which are almost impossible.'[6]

When we come to Margaret Atwood's own work, my impression is that it has less to do with survival than with *regeneration* – a theme that is still, and in a more optimistic vein – relevant to our topic of life and death. I am thinking for instance of *Surfacing* (1972), the novel of a young woman in her quest for her childhood and her family or, rather, her identity, her place in the world. This is acted out against the background of her mother's death in hospital, her father's mysterious disappearance and an abortion she has been through. All the time death is present in one way or another. Also in the way she speaks about her brother: 'This was where he drowned, he got saved only by accident.... If it had happened to me I would have felt there was something special about me, to be raised from the dead like that.'[7] This motif of her brother's drowning presented as more real than his being saved is recurrent, like the blue heron flying gloriously and beautifully alive (p. 63) but taking on a special meaning when it is found dead and hung up as if crucified (pp. 115, 140, etc.). The message seems to be: anything that suffers and is killed instead of us is Christ, particularly the beasts that die that we may live. There is a palpable disgust with the way we kill animals, fish, frogs, to eat or to use in other ways. The conclusion is: 'Anything we could do to the animals we could do to each other: we practised on them first' (pp. 120-21). We can also compare with Atwood's images. A divorce is like an amputation, you survive but there is less of you (p. 42).

The central scene of the novel is where the first person narrator dives into the lake to try and find the solution to the riddle her father has left her in his drawings, apparently of Indian rock carvings which are now below the surface of the water. The answer she gets has, however, more to do with her own enigma, her life lie about her wedding, divorce and the child left with her former husband. So her disappeared, probably dead father directs her to the Indians who 'did not *own* salvation but they had once known where it lived and their signs marked the sacred places, the places where you could learn the truth ... after the failure of logic' (p. 145). What she sees there, in the water, first seems like her drowned brother. Then she realizes it is her own aborted child. The memories of that event now come back to her mind but in a different version from before. She remembers feeling 'emptied, amputated ... they had planted death in me like a seed' (p. 144). In her world which is divided between killers and those killed, she had let them catch this life living inside her. 'I could have said no but I didn't, that made me one of them too, a killer.... Since then I'd carried that death around inside me...' (p. 145).

As a consequence the narrator now feels the need to be forgiven by her lost child in having another. And so the last few pages of the novel are about the possibilities of life in spite of all death machines, in spite of modern civilization which carries death. She reveals to herself – and to us as readers – a life growing naturally out of death.

Another Canadian writer we might, again, associate to here is Margaret Laurence, for instance in her *A Jest of God* (1966). It is about a woman in her thirties living with her mother on the first floor above the undertaker's or, as it is now renamed, the Funeral Parlour. This used to be her father's business and has a special attraction to her as a place of mystery and comfort. So much for the ever-present practical side of death. The outcome of the novel has to do with life and independence growing out of the death – or rather non-being – of the child of her despair and her longing.

If we move back to Australia, where we started, and consider a writer like Patrick White we will find ample scope for this theme. In every novel you can think of it is of major importance, from *The Living and the Dead* at the beginning of his career to his latest one, *Memoirs of the Many in One*. Take for instance *The Tree of Man* (1956) with its down-to-earth business of life, clearing the land, building, cultivating, but also living through the crises, the floods, the fires and the war. At the end, however, we see that life has taken a different shape for Stan, the main character, something that makes the young evangelist, so certain of his life experience, seem as if from another planet. It is not only life that means something entirely different to the two men. With the concept of life goes the concept and meaning of God. And so, when the meaning of life seems to be summed up for Stan in the gob of spittle glittering intensely and personally on the ground like a jewel, he declares *that* to be God – to the dismay of the young evangelist. This is a short while before the old man dies – a moment that is indirectly described as when this obscure, mysterious life grows *transparent* at last – like that gob of spittle.[8]

Among Patrick White's short stories 'Down at the Dump' is interesting for combining the theme of life and death in its ordinary sense with the idea of spiritual life and death. At the centre is dead Daise Morrow on the occasion of her funeral and around her those who are still physically alive, her sister with her councillor husband and daughter, young Meg, a highly respectable family – but also Ossie, that old scabby deadbeat from down the showground whom Daise had taken up with. It emerges that Daise had been very much alive in her days, a generous kind of person, lovable but not conforming to the suburban morality of her sister. But, departing from realism and moving from one mood or register to another White declares that the dead woman is really standing amongst the mourners making the 'loose woman in floral cotton' (p. 36) something of a messenger of good news proclaiming 'that death isn't death, unless it's the death of love'. But of course no one listens or understands, as they are only human. This is the point where we can draw the line of comparison with Joyce in *his* short story 'The Dead' where another dead person implicitly declares the power of love over death.

Before moving on I find it appropriate to bring in a poem. It was published only last year by the young Australian poet Vicky Raymond and is called 'Holiday Girls' referring to a newspaper headline: 'British Holiday Girls in Death Crash'. It describes in a triptych first the girls setting out from the railway station – an exuberantly lively scene with only one indication of what is to follow: the guard at the gate taking the ticket seems to stretch out a hand of bones – like a modern participant in the dance of death. The middle panel represents the death crash itself or the moment immediately after, displaying all the belongings spread out as well as the little that can be seen of the girls just as other objects or bits of machinery. The third part shows, in the lower half, the arrival at the resort, appropriately called Death-on-Sea, with those already dead observed in sardonically earthy positions. Above, a surrealist treatment of extraordinary familiarity representing the trinity protecting the group of girls in the frozen second, laughing and chatting just as the crash occurs.

In spite of the satiric registration of all the petty details which prove the futile interests of human beings, there is a tenderness in the enumeration of them and a compassion that reaches out to those who are recognized among the dead. The poem's very unsentimentality in rendering these scenes of death and dying combined with its wit and vitality makes it a comment not only on death but very much on life.

What I cannot really go into here is the conception of death – and hence of life – among the Inuit of Canada, the Aborigines of Australia or the Maoris of New Zealand. The last-mentioned country cannot entirely be left out, however. A suitable example would be Janet Frame who wrote herself out of mental hospital and has to write in order to survive. I will not now go into her autobiography in several parts, a work that may well come to be regarded among the most significant literary contributions of our century. What I will consider here is her short animal fable, called 'Two Sheep', about a journey to the slaughter house. The first sheep's awareness of their destination allows it to appreciate the warmth of the sun, the beauty of the sky and the freshness of the grass, whereas the second sheep, unaware of their approaching death complains about the heat and the dust. Not until he is loaded on to the truck with all the other sheep does he understand. Looking out through the slits he now discovers the beauty of the hills and the comfortable warmth of the sun.

The first sheep, on the other hand, having seen so clearly death's imminence, gives up struggling and is 'lying exhausted in a corner of the truck' thus giving the impression of being already dead when all the others are unloaded. This is what gives him the opportunity to get away and join another flock. Now it is his turn to feel the discomforts of the journey while the sheep next to him acts his former part of enjoying being alive. That is how the first sheep understands that his companion is aware of being on his way to certain death or, in other words, of the briefness of life. The first sheep draws his conclusions and henceforth is going 'around in circles ... not knowing whether to think that the hills are bare or whether they are green, whether the hawks are scarce or plentiful, whether the sun is friend or foe. Could the effect of one's consciousness of death on one's view of life be more clearly illustrated?

Now taking the step to India I wish to give you a few examples from R.K. Narayan, passing quickly over his third novel, a feminist one from the thirties called *The Dark Room* where the crisis and turning point is the main character's attempted suicide by drowning. She is rescued, however, and begins a humbler life relieved of her wifely duties, but not being able to stay away from her children, she goes back to a life superficially the same as before but without hope of any human dignity. One may wonder whether this return to life should also be seen as a symbolic representation of reincarnation which is, of course, fundamental in a Hindu's view of life and death.

In *The Financial Expert* (1952) Narayan shows in grotesque colours how people watch out for destitutes dying at the roadside. It is good business to beg money for the funeral. Those alive live off the dying and the dead.

A comic treatment of death and funeral is found in *Waiting for the Mahatma* (1955) when the seemingly dead grandmother starts wriggling her toes just as she is to be burnt. She is rather offended by their attempts to get rid of her and decides to leave everything for a complete withdrawal to a wholly sanctified life, that is living for her death. This novel ends with the assassination of Gandhi. What is unusual, or maybe a bit shocking to a Western reader is that this event becomes subservient to the happy ending, the union of the two young people dependent on Gandhi, and who had just had his blessing on their marriage.

Another novel ending in dubious death, although in a different way, is *The Guide* (1958) because there we do not know whether the main character dies as a martyr or whether he just faints away to be revived later.

The most interesting work by Narayan from the point of view of life and death is, however, *The English Teacher*, as the novel was called when it was first published in 1945. The American edition of 1953 is significantly retitled *Grateful to Life and Death*.[9] It is about Narayan's own experiences, as he tells us elsewhere, of his young wife's sudden illness and death, about his sorrow and how, through a medium, he manages to establish contact with his wife in 'an attempt to turn the other side of the medal of existence, which is called death...' (p. 114). The medium will, for instance, write down his dead wife's description of her existence as a timeless one, a life of thought and experience where thought has solidity and power, where things are more intense than on earth and where the greatest ecstasy is in feeling the Divine Light flooding us' (p. 130). Over a long period, with many disappointments when sometimes, in utter despair, he is tempted to suicide, he nevertheless develops a capacity for communicating with his wife without a medium. She, on her side, claims to be able to see him most of the time and occasionally forgets that they are 'in two totally different modes of existence' (p. 152). She urges him to concentration and receptiveness and warns him that even grief creates a barrier between them (p. 155). On one occasion he feels that 'her presence was unmistakeably there. I could sense it [he says]. The darkness of the night was not felt by me. The distance and loneliness were nothing to me. I quickly enjoyed the fact without stirring the slightest thought' (p. 133). At other times he feels desolate: 'The awful irresponsiveness of Death overwhelmed me again' and he asks himself: 'I have been clinging to the veriest straw, thinking that I was on land. Now the straw has snapped and I know my position. I can only drown. I'm drowned, and did not know it all these days. I was clinging to a grass blade at the brink of a well' (p. 149). Gradually he comes to feel that all the things we regard as important are 'trash, we are obliged to go through and pretend that we like them, but all the time the problem of living and dying is crushing us' (p. 149).

Mixed into and contrasted to this process towards an easy and natural communication with his wife comes the story of his friend and schoolmaster, calmly telling him of his belief in an astrologer's report that he is to die the following day. 'This was too disturbing – even for me who had been educated to accept and accommodate the idea of death' (p. 161). When, to the friend's astonishment, the astrologer is found to be wrong or wrongly interpreted, he just states: 'I can't tell you *why* I am alive.... There is no explanation for it, as there is no explanation for death' (p. 167), something that obviously also has wider application.

His little daughter is a source of comfort – but also of worries. It seems best for her to stay with her grandparents in the country leaving him to a solitary life. He bears it stoically thinking:

> There is no escape from loneliness and separation.... Wife, child, brothers, parents, friends.... We come together only to go apart again. It is one continuous movement. They move away from us as we move away from them. The law of life can't be avoided.... A profound unmitigated loneliness is the only truth of life. (p. 177)

The novel ends, however, not on the tone of despair that colours a large part of it. Instead we witness a relaxed moment when he calls for his wife and finds that he can see her, not only talk to her. As they stand together by the window looking at the first purple of the dawn he feels that 'the boundaries of our personalities suddenly dissolved. It was a moment of rare immutable joy – a moment for which one feels grateful to Life and Death' (p. 184). This is the conclusion of a novel praised by many for things like the realistic description of the teacher's wife's illness and death as well as of the aspirations and shortcomings of the teacher. Whatever we may think of the reality of the supernatural experiences of the borderlands where life and death overlap, the fact is that this is Narayan's most closely autobiographical novel.

As for Africa there is an altogether different attitude to death as appears for instance in Chinua Achebe's *Things Fall Apart* (1958). Most clearly it comes out when a great warrior is dead and his funeral celebrated with drums and guns and a show of violence. Particularly the ancestral spirits appearing from the underworld completely covered in raffia and speaking in tremulous, unearthly voices are greatly feared. When this has worked itself up to a climax of noise, tumult, dust and smell the most feared ancestral spirit dances up to the corpse and calls out ritual phrases to the effect that since the dead man had been rich, a fearless warrior and had had a long life, he can only wish him the same kind of conditions when he comes again. Achebe also comments:

> The land of the living was not far removed from the domain of the ancestors. There was coming and going between them, especially at festivals and also when an old man died, because an old man was very close to the ancestors. A man's life from birth to death was a series of transition rites which brought him nearer to his ancestors. (p. 111)

We also see that at a great feast the oldest member of the family is asked to break the kola nut and pray to the ancestors asking them for health and children (p. 151). To Okonkwo, the main character, it is of the utmost importance to have male children who do not desert their old ways by converting to Christianity, thus abandoning their ancestors:

> Okonkwo felt a cold shudder run through him at the terrible prospect of annihilation. He saw himself and his fathers crowding round their ancestral shrine waiting in vain for worship and sacrifice and finding nothing but ashes of bygone days, and his children the while praying to the white man's god. If such a thing were ever to happen, he Okonkwo, would wipe them off the face of the earth. (p. 139)

And so, when Okonkwo takes his own life, it is more than personal despair, it is despair on account of the whole tribe and its traditional way of life and death.

There are, of course, variations even in black African writing, but the belief in a continued existence after death and in the influence of the dead on the lives of the living seems to be general. Another example, also from West Africa and from Nigeria with its 300 million inhabitants but from another people than Achebe's Ibo, i.e. the Yoruba, is one of the earliest black novels from Africa, Amos Tutuola's *The Palm Wine Drinkard*. Here we follow the Drinkard's quest for his dead tapster taking him through mythical and heroic adventures to the Town of the Dead where he goes through initiation tests and rites. That is how he begins to understand the true meaning of death and life, something that will enable him to restore peace and order to his people back home.

Finally we move on to Wilson Harris's *Palace of the Peacock* (1960) where the theme of life and death – life as death, death as life – is present on practically every page. The main action consists of the voyage by boat up the river into the interior of Guyana. It is a journey of life –

but also of death. I cannot help but seeing this in the light of Egyptian mythology, specifically where it deals with the passage on board the boat of death to another world, another life, combining the idea of the sun's passage as we see it during the day and then in darkness back on board the boat of night or death to be able to start it all over again. Wilson Harris makes the same crew that died before undertake the journey again and now they are meeting their death a second time and beyond death reaching their journey's end – the Palace of the Peacock, symbol of eternity. It is precisely because we find this close union of death and life that there can also be a reconciliation between conqueror and conquered, between colonizer and those colonized. Reading this and seeing history treated as a simultaneous process, the present mixed and blurred with the past, we may well be reminded of the T.S. Eliot of *Four Quartets*.

Two quotations from *Palace of the Peacock* will illustrate the closeness of death to life: 'Everyone remembered that not so long ago this self-same crew had been drowned to a man in the rapids below the Mission' (p. 37). 'The whole crew was one spiritual family living and dying together in a common grave out of which they had sprung again from the same soul and womb as it were' (p. 40). We are reminded of Pozzo, in *Waiting for Godot,* realizing: 'They give birth astride a grave' and Vladimir joining in: 'Astride a grave and a difficult birth.'[10] Now, in Beckett, this forcing together of life and death has a thrust of criticism against our way of living, something we will remember also from Joyce, say in 'The Dead' with its exposure of life that is not really lived, of people who exist merely on routine but are not really alive and so making the dead appear as much more of a living force.

It seems to be particularly in the West that death is seen as something negative, something tragic, something almost shameful and deeply private and so not to be talked about. This is also very much present in Australian literature as illustrated by the Matron's hypocritical attitude in *Mr Scobie's Riddle*. It is of interest here to consider the dramatic genre called tragedy which turns from a play on serious topics, with characters of high rank and in a lofty style into denoting a play ending in unhappiness and death. In that sense 'tragedy' and 'tragic' are applied widely outside this specific genre. Comedy, on the other hand, develops from a play about middle class citizens in a realistic style into the opposite of tragedy, a life-preserving genre with a so-called happy ending in the sense that a couple find each other in love and start a new life cycle, a new generation.

Whatever the case, death is the only certainty in this life. It is a centrally human issue and yet it can be looked upon in very different ways. Without generalizing too much – except in so far as to suggest that the very essence of the Commonwealth experience is one of existential crisis, of a lostness in the world and in life – we might see some basic differences between the cultures represented in this paper, specifically in their way of handling mortality. At the same time – possibly due to my choice of examples – it is surprising to see the extent to which consciousness of death gives a deeper meaning to life, almost becoming a life force. We have also seen variations on the theme of survival, and not only in Canadian literature, as well as thoughts of reincarnation. In the reading presented here we can experience the precariousness of life in unexplored countries – unexplored taken either in an absolute or an individual sense – or the merging of life with death in the ultimate oneness of colonizer with colonized. These are some of the attitudes to the matter of life and death that almost by definition have arisen out of the Commonwealth condition.

NOTES

1. Elizabeth Jolley, *Mr Scobie's Riddle* (Victoria: Penguin Books Australia, 1983), p. 120.
2. As far as I can see, the idea of survival as the central and decisive symbol of Canada goes back to Northrop Frye.
3. Margaret Atwood, *Survival* (Toronto: Anansi, 1972), p. 33.
4. Robert Weaver and William Toye, eds., *The Oxford Anthology of Canadian Literature* (Toronto University Press, 1973), p. 251.
5. Margaret Atwood, *Survival*, p. 34.
6. Margaret Laurence, as quoted in *The Oxford Anthology of Canadian Literature*, pp. 439-40.
7. Margaret Atwood, *Surfacing* (1972; London: Virago, 1979), p. 74.
8. Patrick White, *The Tree of Man* (1956; Harmondsworth: Penguin, (1961) 1972), pp. 476-8.
9. R.K. Narayan, *The English Teacher* (London: Eyre and Spottiswoode, 1945), p. 184.
10. Samuel Beckett, *Waiting for Godot* (1955; London: Faber, 1959) pp. 89, 91; cf. Jeremiah 20:17-18.

NOTES ON CONTRIBUTORS

Jennifer Breen teaches at the North London Polytechnic and has published criticism mainly on Australian literature.

John Colmer is retired Professor of English at the University of Adelaide and has published widely on Patrick White, Australian biography, etc.

David Dabydeen teaches Caribbean literature at the University of Warwick. He has published poetry and criticism.

Kacke Götrick wrote her doctoral dissertation on African drama. She teaches at the department of Swedish literature in Lund.

Karin Hansson wrote her doctoral dissertation on Patrick White and teaches at the University of Lund.

Kirsten Holst Petersen teaches at the University of Aarhus and has published widely in the field of post-colonial studies.

Stephan Larsen wrote his doctoral thesis on Wole Soyinka and is currently working at a comparative study of African literature in French and English.

Ganeswar Mishra is Professor and Head of the Department of English at Utkal University, Bhubaneswar, India. He has written mainly on Indian literature.

Prafulla Mohanti is an architect, painter and writer dividing his life between London and Orissa, India. His native village plays a central part in his writing.

Alastair Niven has taught at universities in Scotland and Africa. He was Director of the Africa Centre, London, and is at present Director of Literature for the British Arts Council.

Britta Olinder wrote her doctoral dissertation on 17th century drama, has published in the field of post-colonial literatures, and teaches at Gothenburg University.

Peter Porter is a literary critic and one of the most important Australian poets today. His *Collected Poems* appeared in 1984. He lives in London.

Vicki Raymond is an administrator and another Australian poet abroad. Her first collection of poetry won her a Commonwealth Poetry Prize.

Anna Rutherford from Australia is Professor of English at the University of Aarhus. She has published and edited widely in the field of post-colonial literatures, and she is editor of the journal *Kunapipi*.

Rudy Wiebe teaches Canadian literature and creative writing at the University of Alberta, Edmonton. Among his many works of fiction and of the history of Western Canada *Playing Dead* is the most recent one.